BOWHUNTING
FORESTS & DEEP WOODS

by Greg Miller

P.O. Box 1148, Chanhassen, MN 55317-1148

Our toll-free number to place an order is **(866) 837-3135**. Please use our regular business telephone (952) 949-2800 for further information about other IHUNT Communications books like "Life at Full Draw, The Chuck Adams Story."

Photos by Greg Miller
Book design by Whitedog Design Company

ISBN 0-9721321-2-0

10 9 8 7 6 5 4 3 2 1

Printed in the United States of America

ISBN:0-972132-2-0

8 24274 01995 3

THIS BOOK AIDS THE BOWHUNTING PRESERVATION ALLIANCE

Your purchase of this book helps protect and preserve bowhunting. The Bowhunting Preservation Alliance (BPA), a nonprofit foundation created by the Archery Trade Association, has underwritten the costs of "Bowhunting Forests & Deep Woods." The BPA and author Greg Miller hope your enjoyment of this book will be increased by knowing that you helped save and strengthen bowhunting.

The BPA — www.bowhuntingpreservation.org — was formed in 2002 to be a strong, unwavering advocate for bowhunting, hunting and conservation. Its main objectives include recruiting new bowhunters while retaining experienced bowhunters. To do this, the BPA strives to provide leadership and vision while building strong alliances among and between the archery and bowhunting industry, bowhunting organizations, and state and federal agencies across North America.

The BPA's president and CEO is Jay McAninch, a former wildlife biologist in New York and Minnesota. "BPA is working to increase bowhunting oportunities, enhance public awareness about bowhunting, lower barriers to bowhunting, and unite bowhunters and bowhunting organizations," McAninch said. "The Archery Trade Association has agreed to cover the overhead costs for the BPA, which means every dollar we raise, including from this book, go directly to support a bowhunting project."

McAninch said bowhunters like Greg Miller understand the importance of helping the BPA meet its objectives. McAninch said: "Greg is a straight-shooting guy who will work with us to make a lasting impact on bowhunting, and he insists on account-ability. Not only is the BPA working directly with individuals like Greg, we're also capturing federal funds and grant money to build and improve archery ranges and bowhunter education programs across the country."

For more information about the BPA, contact:
Bowhunting Preservation Alliance
304 Brown St. East, Box 258
Comfrey, MN 56019
www.bowhuntingpreservation.org
Toll-free (866) 266-2776; or (507) 877-5300

This book is
dedicated to
Jerry Lahner and
Adam Stuckert,
a couple of true
big-woods
bowhunting
pioneers.

ACKNOWLEDGMENTS

I must first thank my dad for introducing me to big-woods whitetail hunting. Those first hunts with him so many years ago kindled a fire within me that still burns hot!

I also must thank some of the more special big-woods hunting partners I've had over the years. This list includes people like my brothers Mike, Jim and Jeff; and friends like Swede, Dan Dyson, Gabby and Kevin Shibilski, to name but a few.

And, finally, I'd like to thank my son, Jake, for his companionship in the forests and deep woods during his early years as a bowhunter. You'll never know, Son, just how proud I was that you were so eager to accept the big-woods challenge.

INTRODUCTION

I easily remember the day my good friend Patrick Durkin approached me with a proposal to write a book on bowhunting whitetails in the forests and deep woods. I also remember that, although I didn't tell Pat at the time, I initially had some trepidations about writing such a book. I wasn't worried about coming up with enough good information. Rather, I was more concerned whether the book would have broad enough "reader appeal."

Those fears disappeared quickly as I started piling up the chapters. As I wrote, I realized more than ever that this is the kind of material many people ask me about whenever I'm on the phone or giving a seminar. As Pat told me recently: "There's a lot of good stuff in this book, Greg. You tackled the subject with your usual no-nonsense approach."

I take Pat's words as a generous compliment. Not only that, but that's the approach I was hoping to project in this book. You see, it's my opinion that bowhunting big-woods whitetails must be viewed as a no-nonsense endeavor — at least while you're in the big timber.

To put it bluntly, this kind of bowhunting ain't for everyone! Chasing mature white-tailed bucks in big-woods habitats is a unique challenge. What do I consider big woods? At the minimum, we're talking about timber that covers 320 acres. In many cases, of course, we're dealing with thousands of acres of unbroken forest land. You can expect a few small openings within that cover, of course, but never do you find extensive fields like those so common in farm country. In fact, it's possible you'll find only miles of timber between one road and the next in some of North America's public and corporate forests.

What that means, of course, is that getting "visuals" of big bucks can be extremely tough. For that matter, consistent sightings of *any* deer are often major accomplishments. But like any true dyed-in-the-wool big-woods bowhunter, I love the challenges associated with chasing mature whitetails in such country. The sense of accomplishment one feels when succeeding in the big woods can shoot off the charts.

Obviously, I've deeply appreciated each of the mature bucks I've tagged in my lifetime, but I admit I take special pride in my big-woods successes. They remain especially memorable.

— *Greg Miller, Bloomer, Wis., October 2004*

One morning in 1994 while deer hunting in northwestern Ontario, I heard several gunshots from the direction where I had parked my truck. Later, as I walked back toward the truck around lunchtime, I heard birds making a commotion up ahead near the logging road. Soon I spotted ravens and gray jays hopping about in the treetops and circling above, all of them sounding irritated. After sneaking ahead a few steps toward a clearing by the road, I saw a bald eagle sitting astride a mountainous gut pile from a freshly killed moose. All those birds obviously resented the eagle's intrusion and were letting him know it.

Personally, I didn't know what was more intriguing: the big eagle or the enormous gut pile providing his food. When my eyes locked with the eagle's, his gaze felt oddly familiar. Before the eagle flew off in surprise, I smiled in recognition: the predator eye. I knew those eyes well. I had long joked that Greg Miller, in an earlier life, was an eagle or a wolf.

By the time of that encounter with the bald eagle, I had been friends with Greg more than three years, but I had known of him much longer. When we first met in April 1991, I was struck by the intensity in his eyes, which size up everything around him with fierce directness. In fact, I could picture Miller up in his tree stand, silent and alert, head on a swivel, peering down on a buck much like an eagle sizing up a rabbit.

And like the bald eagle, Miller seems most at home in "the big woods," which means the sprawling forests, big timber and deep woods from the southeastern United States to Alberta, Canada. Sure, he's equally adept at bowhunting farm country and Western river bottoms, but Miller just seems part of the natural order in lands inhabited by wolves, coyotes, fishers, bobcats and/or black bears.

Some deer hunters don't have the patience to hunt such areas because deer numbers in forests and deep woods can be lower than they like, and deer can hide almost everywhere. Still, bowhunters know long waits and hard work are worth the rewards when they're standing over a mature, deep-chested, heavy-antlered forest buck.

That's why Miller has spent most of his life enduring the frozen hands, frosted feet and long walks often required for serious big-woods bowhunting. He prides himself on being one of a rare breed who hunts such regions regularly, and on being one of an even rarer breed who enjoys consistent success on the forest's most impressive bucks.

Perhaps his determination helps explain why Greg Miller has developed such an intense following among white-tailed deer hunters. His blue-collar, workmanlike approach strikes a chord with bowhunters, who also appreciate his direct, no-nonsense answers to every question he hears. If you're looking for shortcuts to success or endorsements of dubious products, you're asking the wrong man. That's not Miller's style.

His word matters. As do his skills and experience. He would probably describe himself as an overachiever, a guy of "regular" skills who just works harder than most, but he is also a quick-studied analyst with confidence in his skills and insights. In addition, he has the utmost respect for whitetails, which makes him strive more than most bowhunters to avoid detection. Miller might say all those things are true, but would add that one must never underestimate the whitetail, and that means scouting and analyzing deer sign whenever possible.

That's one of the many messages Miller delivers in this, his fifth book. Inside these pages you'll find more than 40 years of Miller's big-woods expertise bundled into one convenient package. You can read it at bedtime, in your deer camp at midday, and maybe even in your tree stand. But if you think you can then just go out and apply all the new information you've absorbed, think again. If Miller were nearby when you finish reading, he would probably put an arm over your shoulders, fix his predator eyes on yours, and say: "Time to start scouting. Let's go wear down some shoe leather."

As with any other good teacher, Miller knows he can't do your bowhunting for you. This book can make you better understand the woods and provide new tactics, but you can't apply the knowledge effectively if you don't learn your hunting land and the deer that live there.

Once you do that, the book will prove even more invaluable.

— *Patrick Durkin*
Contributing Editor, Bowhunting Preservation Alliance

CHAPTER ONE

THE FOREST & DEEP-WOODS CHALLENGE

As many bowhunters can attest, nothing matches the sense of accomplishment we get from taking a mature white-tailed buck. It doesn't matter what level of difficulty we overcame, either. Harvesting a big buck with the bow and arrow is a major accomplishment, no matter the circumstances.

Even so, take it from someone who has bowhunted mature bucks across much of North America: The toughest habitat for bowhunting big bucks is the big woods. Those who know me probably think I'm biased. After all, my first deer hunts — which date back to the mid-1960s — took place in wilderness areas of northwestern Wisconsin. And, yes, memories of those big-woods hunts help explain my infatuation with chasing whitetails in such environments. Those same memories, however, reinforce my belief that achieving consistent success on trophy-class white-tails in the big woods is the toughest ticket going.

LIGHTING THE FIRE

The Wisconsin forest I first hunted remains a big-woods environment to this day, but it's not nearly as vast as it was 40 years ago. My link to this area came through my father, who chipped in $100 to help 11 friends and relatives buy a cabin and 40 acres of land about 12 miles north of Danbury in 1949.

My first trips to the North Woods took place during Wisconsin's nine-day gun season, which runs through Thanksgiving week. Though I was only 12 on my first trip to the "Stuckert Deer Camp," I soon realized those nine days weren't enough time to chase whitetails. Thanks to a couple of Dad's fel-

Those who specialize in big-woods bowhunts often trace their roots to family traditions and old-time deer camps. This 1949 photo shows the author's father and members of his Wisconsin deer camp, a setting where Greg Miller got his start in deer hunting in the 1960s. In case you're wondering about this meat-pole, Wisconsin mandated antlerless-only hunting for the 1949 gun season.

low shareholders, Adam Stuckert and Jerry Lahner, I discovered an option. Those men were the first serious bowhunters I met. Even more importantly, they spent a lot of time chasing white-tails in many of the same areas we gun-hunted in late November.

I remember my boyhood awe listening to Adam and Jerry talk about their bowhunts. Hunting success was hard-won in those forests, even with a firearm. As a result, I struggled to believe anyone could ambush a big-woods deer with the bow and arrow. Even so, I wanted to give it a shot.

I only had to wait a couple of years to realize my dream of chasing big-woods whitetails with a bow. Those first bowhunts didn't take place near Dad's cabin, but they still were big-woods adventures in all respects. My brother Mike had a friend with a cabin 15 miles north of our hometown, Bloomer, Wis. The cabin was smack dab in the middle of one of the area's largest blocks of timber. We had thousands of acres of roadless forest to bowhunt.

13

Greg Miller's father had two close friends who piqued the boy's early interest in big-woods bowhunting. These men were part of a northern Wisconsin gun camp, but they spent far more time chasing whitetails earlier each fall with bows and arrows. This photo shows their camp during the 1950 gun season. The author's father is in the back row, third from left.

We thought we had the keys to heaven!

Mike's friend shared our passion for bowhunting whitetails, as did several other guys our age we picked up along the way. Oh sure, we kept terrorizing cottontails with our beagles, and we derived other pleasures from hunting squirrels, grouse and waterfowl. But no other type of hunting measured up to chasing deer with the "stick and string." That was especially true during the rut.

EARLY EDUCATION

Some experiences during my first couple of years of bowhunting helped shape my lifelong approach to deer hunting. One influential aspect of that early education is something I call the "intimidation factor." This is the fear and uncertainty hunters often feel when considering how to hunt huge chunks of roadless cover.

I won't play Mr. Macho and claim I've never been scared off by a sprawling forest. At first I feared the prospect of walking into roadless timber that stretched for miles. Those fears kept me fairly close to the roads. My next step was to tag along with my older brother or one of his buddies when they explored haunts farther from the roads.

Eventually I realized I needed my own system for finding my way into and out of our favorite big-woods sites. My first step was learning to use a compass. As time went by, I also learned the nuances of using the sun to keep my bearings. It helped that, like many good woodsmen, I had a reasonably accurate sense of direction. Over the years I've honed this inner sense.

My training in big-woods navigation received a boost during my second season. On a snowy mid-November morning, one of our guys wounded a big buck. The six of us who were hunting that day jumped in on the trailing job. Over the next five hours the deer took us on an intimate journey through its stomping grounds. By the time we caught up to this buck — an 8-pointer with a 19½-inch spread — he had provided valuable insights into the habits of big-woods whitetails.

Our education that day in 1966 was helped greatly by 4 inches of fresh snow. The snow increased visibility, which allowed us to study a lot more country than usual. The snow also helped us study the tracks of other deer whose paths we crossed while trailing the buck. Even though I was a youngster, it didn't take long to figure out there was one heck of a lot of country these whitetails didn't use much!

Remember, too, this hunt took place long before we had "specialty" magazines devoted to hunting trophy whitetails. Likewise, so-called big-buck experts had not yet been created by videos, TV shows and magazines. Few hunters knew the intricacies of using topographical maps and aerial photos as year-round scouting aids and shortcuts to locating big-buck hangouts. But even with those reference aids, nothing tells you more about whitetail country than walking every square foot of it!

15

BOWHUNTING FORESTS & DEEP WOODS

IT AIN'T EASY

I'm often asked why I love bowhunting big-woods whitetails. For one thing, my hunting and bowhunting roots sprouted from the big woods, as did my family's. In fact, their roots had grown deeply long before I entered the scene. Therefore, it was a natural progression for me to follow the footsteps of my father, grandfather, an uncle and a slew of cousins.

However, my passion for chasing big-woods whitetails involves more than tradition. In a sense, and to quote a friend, big-woods deer hunters are born, not made. Of course, one doesn't require a family tradition of big-woods hunting to be born a big-woods fanatic. I know dozens of successful bowhunters whose families never set foot in the big woods. Still, they took to the task with a passion and intensity that sets them apart from other hunters. Chasing big-woods whitetails is in their blood.

Bowhunting big-woods trophies includes unique challenges. Deer numbers are almost always far lower than in most habitats, and they're usually scattered in pockets throughout many miles of cover. As a result, frustration hounds many bowhunters. One source of frustration is the whitetail's feeding preferences. Unlike farmlands, most big-woods deer foods are disguised within the timber, often unrecognized by casual hunters. In agricultural areas, one need only pay attention to crop foods and where they're planted. Once you pinpoint such spots it's just a matter of scouting to find how deer approach and leave their feeding areas.

Besides obvious big-woods deer foods — such as fresh browse from logging — most concentrated feeding areas are difficult to locate. It's doubtful you'll find a hot feeding area by driving around in your truck or ATV. To achieve consistent success as a big-woods bowhunter, you must pull on your favorite walking boots and put them to work.

I'm often asked how big-woods deer respond to human activity, including the wanderings of scouting hunters. Many hunters ask if these whitetails differ from their farmland cousins. My answer is a resounding "yes." I believe those differences are day and night, with the most significant difference being their reaction to humans and anything they might associate with human activity.

Big-woods bucks seldom fall to bowhunters who aren't excellent woodsmen. A critical step in consistent big-woods bowhunting success is learning how to navigate in forests and large woods. Such settings can intimidate those who spend most of their time in small woodlots and patch-work farmland woods.

For instance, I recall a hunt years ago when I was sitting on a stand nearly a half-mile from the nearest road. It was roughly an hour before dark, and I was deep in thought when I heard deer approaching. A doe and two fawns soon strolled into view. When they were within 20 yards they began feeding on acorns. I watched their back-trail for several minutes, but didn't see or hear evidence of a trailing buck, so I relaxed and studied the doe and fawns.

17

Although many top big-woods bowhunters are born into the tradition, such pedigrees aren't mandatory. The author knows many good bowhunters who fell in love with the big-woods challenge on their own. They cherish the experience as much as those whose family tree is rooted in the big woods.

The day was clear, calm and cool — perfect conditions for carrying sound seemingly forever. About 15 minutes after the deer appeared, I heard a car door slam on the distant road. All three deer snapped their heads erect and stared that way. A few seconds later I heard faint talking. I didn't have to look to confirm if the deer heard the voices. They turned, and with flared tails, bounded into thick cover.

This is just one of hundreds of experiences I've had that illustrate the flighty, paranoid behavior of big-woods deer. Older deer, especially mature bucks, have little tolerance for any human activity. Unlike farmland deer, they seldom display any curiosity when encountering human sounds and activity.

Couple that trait with low deer numbers, and you better understand the need for persistence. Although 40 years have passed since my indoctrination to bowhunting, I recall Adam Stuckert and Jerry Lahner discussing the rarity of deer sightings. As Adam said: "In this country it's not unusual to go for days without seeing a deer. That can make it difficult to return, but Jerry and I keep coming back. There's something special about bowhunting the big woods."

Many years went by before I really understood what Adam meant. But after four more years of high school and four years of military service, including duty in Vietnam — where I constantly dreamed of chasing whitetails — I started bowhunting big-woods bucks. It took only a few hunts to realize Adam was right. It was indeed special.

A BAD CHANGE

Unfortunately, that special feeling has been tougher to find near home in recent years. Why? Some people do all they can to create shortcuts to the big woods' secrets. That's why I have spent little time bowhunting Wisconsin's North Woods since the late 1990s. I must go elsewhere to enjoy my passion. It's not that I can't hunt the forests of my youth. Rather, it's that other people denied me that privilege when they fell hard for deer baiting. As deer baiting grew ever more popular in Wisconsin's North Woods after the late 1980s, my enthusiasm for bowhunting those big woods decreased proportionately.

My big-woods bowhunting success is tightly linked to the

Although driving around in a truck or car lets you see some great whitetail country, don't expect to find a big-woods feeding area from behind the wheel. These gems are usually located where motor vehicle travel is impossible or extremely risky. You're better off scouting on foot once you've pinpointed which area you'll hunt.

time and effort I spend learning which natural foods deer eat at specific times in autumn. And trust me, it takes tremendous effort and analysis to piece together a forest deer's autumn diet. I worked many years as a construction worker and chased whitetails whenever I wasn't sporting a hard hat. As a result, like most blue-collar workers, I did most of my hunting and scouting on weekends. Despite such time constraints, I eventually figured out the foods deer keyed on one week to the next. And, yes, those preferences sometimes changed that quickly.

When deer baiters took over northwestern Wisconsin, they decapitated my style of hunting. All the work I had done to pinpoint those ever-changing food preferences became irrelevant. Deer no longer had to work for their food. Instead of staying on their hoofs for long periods to search out forbs, lichens, buds, leaves, acorns and woody browse to fill their bellies, deer simply

The author believes farmland whitetails are much more tolerant of human intrusions than are big-woods deer. While farmland deer expect humans to show up occasionally, big-woods deer sense something is amiss and instantly lie low when humans intrude.

found the nearest corn or sugar-beet pile, and then rested near-by to chew their cud and digest their hand-delivered meals.

I won't debate the ethics of baiting or its potential for spread-ing communicable diseases. I will, however, say it's not my way to hunt deer, and I hate the way it changed the behavioral and travel patterns of big-woods whitetails I once hunted. And it's not that I couldn't exploit those new patterns, but doing so can cause trouble with those ladling out the bait. The Wisconsin forests I long hunted are publicly owned, yet baiters act as if their corn pile is a legal claim to the surrounding 40 acres. As a result, game wardens must handle repeated calls to settle disputes over hunt-ing rights on public land. It's a sad commentary on the times.

Even so, these affairs haven't dampened my enthusiasm for bowhunting the big woods in other locales. If anything, the chal-lenges of figuring out new big-woods areas fuels my hunting fires even more. From the mid-1990s through the time this book was written (2004), I've discovered several intriguing big-woods environments across North America. As were the big-woods regions of northern Wisconsin before baiting became rampant, most of these "new" stomping grounds are under-hunted.

THE PRESSURE FACTOR

In summary, I'll elaborate on the importance of low hunting pressure. Many factors make bowhunting the big woods for tro-phy whitetails a tough gig. However, the one factor working to the hunter's advantage is low hunting pressure. I've hunted the big woods in a half-dozen states and three provinces, and hunt-ing pressure has always been light. This is a huge plus when you're hunting mature white-tailed bucks. Low hunting pres-sure allows you to single out and hunt individual bucks without worrying about interference from other hunters.

With this introductory chapter, I've barely scratched the sur-face about becoming a proficient big-woods bowhunter. The chap-ters that follow give an in-depth look at the what, when, where, how and why of consistent success. Be forewarned, it's a huge challenge in all respects, but that's why it's so alluring.

The author believes deer baiting, even where legal, dramatically changes feeding and behavioral patterns of big-woods whitetails. Artificial food sites that get replenished regularly cause deer to bed nearby and travel less often.

CHAPTER TWO

DEFINING DEEP WOODS

Before going further into this book, let's answer an obvious question: What exactly do I mean when talking about the "big woods?" My many talks with deer hunters over the years remind me that there's a wealth of opinions on this matter.

I heard one such view while talking with a fellow hunter at a Wisconsin deer show. The young man and I had been talking awhile about scouting, stand placement, hunting pressure, deer densities and the effectiveness of morning vs. evening hunts. As we talked, it finally dawned on me that he was actually hunting farmland woodlots.

"I thought you said you were hunting the big woods," I said pleasantly. He paused, looked at me with a puzzled expression and said: "I am. The deer I'm hunting live in a huge woodlot that's about dead-center in the middle of my property. I'm guessing, but I'd say the woods covers close to 100 acres. That's a pretty big woods!"

I had to agree with the guy, to some extent. One-hundred acres of unbroken timber with no roads is a hefty chunk of ground these days in the upper Midwest. But it doesn't begin to describe my definition of "big woods." When I talk about the big woods, I'm thinking in terms of thousands of acres, not hundreds. In fact, I can think of a few big-woods hunts when I've talked in terms of square miles, not acres.

For the sake of this book, let's agree a big woods must feature, at bare minimum, 320 acres of unbroken timber, wherever whitetails are found. It could be the large public forests of the Great Lakes region and Western provinces; the far Northeastern states; the Adirondacks, Appalachians and Allegheny regions; Southern mountains and swamps; or any large commercial forests, North or South.

Severe winters and abundant four-legged predators do their part to keep deer numbers in check in many large North Woods habitats in Northern states and Western provinces.

When the author uses the term "big woods," he's talking of woodlands that cover thousands of acres, not hundreds of acres. The "big woods" cover at least 320 acres of unbroken terrain, and are part of much larger blocks of large woods and forest.

That isn't to say big-woods environments don't exist in farm country. They do, of course. In fact, I've hunted some big woods in southwestern Wisconsin near the Mississippi River. One such area, Buffalo County, has produced more Boone and Crockett entries than any county in North America. Furthermore, some deer hunters mistakenly believe big woods can only be found in Northern states and Canada. They equate "big woods" with wilderness areas, and believe the habitat must hold lynx, bobcats, fishers, coyotes, black bears or timber wolves, and mile upon mile of unbroken forest.

Obviously, some big woods feature wilderness, but most North American big woods are tamer and considerably smaller. About the only four-legged predators you'll often find in abundance are coyotes and bobcats, depending on the location. Still, the forests cover large swaths of country and meet my definition of "big woods."

OVERLOOKED GEMS?

My hunts for trophy whitetails have taken me throughout North America. As I drive, I keep my eyes open for areas that look worthy of follow-up investigation. I pay close attention whenever I see vast areas of unbroken ground. Two areas that piqued my interest in recent years are the Shawnee National Forest in southern Illinois and the Hoosier State Forest in southern Indiana. These huge forests feature extensive stretches of unbroken timber, and steep, rugged terrain. One glance told me the Shawnee and Hoosier forests have everything needed to produce giant whitetails.

Although I haven't hunted either forest, I've talked to others who have. They confirmed what I suspected: Deer numbers are average, hunting pressure is light to nonexistent, and the quality of top-end bucks killed in recent years is off the charts. Those are the usual traits of a big woods with whitetails!

I would be remiss to not mention Michigan's Upper Peninsula, because it's the epitome of what a big woods should look like. This region features mile after mile of forests, much of it dissected by fast-flowing, crystal-clear trout streams. The terrain varies from flatlands with mere 5-foot elevation changes, to hilly and rugged ridges that make you sweat and gasp.

As much as I admire the U.P. when driving through, I've never hunted it. In talking with friends who often hunted there I know deer numbers are relatively low across much of the peninsula, and extensive baiting causes problems similar to those seen in Wisconsin, which we discussed in Chapter 1. The U.P. also has a tradition of severe winters, with deep snow and many sub-zero days. Snow often arrives in late October through mid-November, and can stay around until mid-April to early May. As a result, the U.P. sustains some whitetail winterkill nearly every year, and some years the toll is frightening. In addition, a growing population of timber wolves inhabit the U.P., and they can eat a lot of deer, especially during severe winters and at fawning time.

In all respects, the U.P. can be a harsh environment. Across much of this land, U.P. deer are as apt to die through natural selection as they are from an arrow or bullet. But that's not necessarily a bad thing. The sick, the young, the old, the weak, the crippled and the rut-weary often succumb to weather, wolves or black bears, depending on the season. Black bears have been shown to prey heavily on newborn fawns each May and June, and rut-depleted bucks are the first to go in harsh winters. That's nature's way.

Even so, the strong, crafty and fortunate survive, which increases the likelihood that the herd's healthiest and heartiest individuals do most of the breeding. Although the U.P. can't boast a large herd, it's home to some stud bucks! And, by the way, most of them live on land that's open to public hunting, because the U.P. contains huge tracts of federal, state, county and corporate forests.

OH, CANADA!

Speaking of harsh winters and abundant predators, it seems fitting to discuss Canada's big woods. I've chased whitetails in Alberta, Saskatchewan and Manitoba, and loved every minute of it!

As with Michigan's U.P. — and northern Minnesota, for that matter — much of Canada's "bush" country exemplifies what the big woods are all about. These lands feature low deer densities, lots of predators, little to no hunting pressure, and miles of

Bowhunting Canada's big woods, or "bush," is a great experience. These hunts can be expensive and require large investments of time for travel, but don't be surprised if you find yourself making repeated sacrifices to return for more fun.

unbroken forests. In other words, paradise for a passionate big-woods hunter. Believe it or not, much of the "bush" remains as wild today as it was when I first hunted it more than 15 years ago.

Even so, bowhunting in Canada isn't pain-free. With rare exceptions — such as parts of northwestern Ontario — U.S. residents must hire a licensed hunting guide or outfitter. Perhaps more daunting, however, is simple logistics. Even from my home in northwestern Wisconsin, I'm still a long drive away from Canada's top whitetail range.

29

The author and his brother Jeff have bowhunted Manitoba's Spruce Woods National Forest several times. This area boasts some tremendous whitetails and features habitat that reminds them of their North Woods haunts in Wisconsin.

That can be a real issue, especially for bowhunting. If you're like me, you must pack a lot of gear and equipment. An extra bow is a must. I also want my own tree stands. Throw in a few dozen tree steps, and varied footwear and clothing so you're prepared for everything from balmy weather to arctic blasts, and you've eliminated the possibility of flying to your destination. I hope you're prepared to spend a couple of days behind the wheel!

By now the cash register in your head should be starting to ring. Bowhunting Canada ain't cheap! Whether you drive or fly, you'll quickly spend $3,000 for the Canadian experience!

Is it worth it? I can't answer that for you, but I'll offer a warning: It took me nearly three years to save up for my first bowhunt in Canada. I told myself it would be a once-in-a-lifetime trip. That notion flew out the window before my hunt was half over. I was back two years later for two bowhunts: one to Alberta and one to Manitoba. By 2003 I had been to Canada 14 times. For me, Canada is an addiction. The same thing might happen to you. Don't say I didn't warn you!

As much as I love hunting there, I never forget this fact: Canada is a foreign country. Be prepared to have your vehicle, baggage and packages torn apart at the border when entering Canada or returning to the United States. If you're singled out for "the treatment," keep your cool. And if you're fortunate enough to harvest a whitetail, make sure your license, export permit and other paperwork is in order before entering Customs. To be safe, also carry a copy of your birth certificate. The more you're prepared, the less likely you'll experience unnecessary delays.

FARMLANDS AND FRINGE COUNTRY

If you think Canada is the only region with big-woods brutes, you might miss out on great hunts closer to home. For instance, I often hunt a couple of great sites in Buffalo County, Wisconsin. The big woods in the Bluff Country — which also includes Pepin and Trempealeau counties — have their own unique make-up. Although active farms still dot the countryside, Mother Nature has reclaimed many of the old family-run operations.

Not only are some blocks of timber much larger than 320 acres, the terrain in these extensive woods is steep and rugged. Granted, these hills aren't the Appalachians or Adirondacks, but they'll cause problems for hunters who aren't in shape. Those problems fade quickly, however, when you consider the quantity and quality of the region's bucks. These sprawling woods, rugged terrain and self-imposed antler restrictions by local hunters ensure many trophy bucks roam the region.

I'm sure other parts of North America feature terrain similar to Wisconsin's Bluff Country, which at first glance appears relatively easy to scout and hunt. Well, I admit it might not be difficult to figure it out, but hunting this country is a different story, and I'll discuss it in depth later in this book.

I dub this type of big woods "Fringe Country." In brief, this is where agricultural lands end and large expanses of forest cover begin. We have many such areas in Wisconsin, and I've seen similar fringe-country habitats in Minnesota, Michigan and Canada. I also know they can be found in upper New York state and in some Western states.

I've bowhunted many fringe areas since the early 1990s, and I wish I could boast a modest success rate. But I can't! It's rare for me to throw my hands into the air in frustration, but I've done so several times when bowhunting fringe country.

Let's review some of the reasons for those failures. For starters, whitetails in these areas — including even the most mature bucks — often are visible in crop fields during late summer. But bucks soon disappear after shedding their antler velvet. And I mean they disappear! I seldom find fresh buck sign near the edges of agricultural lands.

Even so, the bucks are usually somewhere nearby. Unfortunately, "somewhere" could be hundreds or even thousands of forested acres. In more traditional big-woods haunts, deer can appear almost nomadic. Fringe-country whitetails take that trait to the next level. In early fall they often relocate some distance back into the woods, away from agricultural grounds. In mid-fall it's possible they will move again. And they might relocate yet again during the pre-rut. Heaven only knows where they'll be when the rut kicks into gear.

I remember an experience several years ago with a huge fringe-country 10-pointer. My brother Jeff and I first saw the buck in late August when it ran across a back-country road a few feet from the front bumper of Jeff's vehicle. We saw the buck again a week later less than a quarter-mile from the first sighting. Then it pulled a classic disappearing act.

Jeff and I bowhunted the area hard during the next couple of months. Not once did we lay eyes on the big 10-pointer. Then, during a morning bowhunt about three miles away, I saw the trophy again. It was late October, which is the peak of pre-rut activity in Wisconsin. I set up over an active scrape/rub line along the edge of a tamarack swamp. I had seen only one deer, a small buck, which appeared shortly after daylight. As 10 o'clock approached, I decided to end my hunt so I wouldn't be late for an appointment in town. I lowered my bow and then did something that still haunts me: I decided to pull my stand from the

The author defines "fringe country" as regions where agricultural habitat ends and the big timber begin. This type of country can be extremely tough to figure out because the whitetails' movements vary considerably depending on their food sources.

The author was stumped by a buck that disappeared without a trace one fall. It showed up three miles away one morning after the author lowered his bow to the ground. When the buck suddenly showed up and walked into range, all the author could do was watch in open-mouthed awe as the 10-pointer worked a couple of scrapes, lip-curled, and then rub-urinated down its hocks.

34

tree. I intended to move to a "hot" cluster of scrapes I had discovered while walking in that morning.

When my bow reached the ground I untied the tow rope and dropped it. I had just stepped off my stand and onto the first tree step when I noticed movement about 50 yards away. You guessed it: The movement was a big buck, and it was heading straight at me! There was no time to climb down and grab my bow, so I climbed back onto my stand, dug out my binoculars and focused on the buck.

Within seconds the buck was 15 yards away, savagely working a licking branch. I didn't need binoculars to confirm this was the buck Jeff and I had seen earlier that fall. His unique and matching "crab-claw" G-4 tines made him easy to identify. I watched in open-mouthed awe as the brute whitetail worked a couple of scrapes, performed a lip curl and then urinated down its hocks. Then it walked in even closer!

At 10 yards the buck stopped and beat the daylights out of a small clump of tag alders. After that he surveyed his surroundings for a half-minute and then snapped his head erect to look right at me! The big 10-pointer did several head-bobs, trying to get me to move. Eventually he must have concluded I posed no threat, so he flicked his tail and walked off into the tamaracks. I never saw him again.

Remember, that encounter occurred three miles from where Jeff and I first saw the buck. I wouldn't have been as surprised if the rut had been in full swing, but it wasn't. In fact, the rut didn't kick into gear until nearly a week later.

This story also highlights one of the pluses of hunting fringe areas. Because deer often flock to croplands during late summer, it's possible to get a partial inventory of bucks in the vicinity. All that's left to figure out is which parts of the nearby big woods they're using at specific times of bow season.

That's why I believe the big woods of fringe country demand the most scouting of all forested environments. Fringe-country bucks seem less apt to restrict their off-rut home range to one particular area. That's another aspect of big-woods deer behavior we'll explore later in more detail.

CHAPTER THREE

ARE YOU MENTALLY PREPARED?

I can honestly say forest and deep-woods deer hunting ran thick and rich through my veins long before I reached legal hunting age, which is 12 in Wisconsin. I waited with great anticipation for Dad to come home from his "up north" deer hunts each November. I would then listen with wide eyes and closed mouth — unusual for me — as he related his latest hunting adventures from the North Woods. And they truly were adventures in those days!

It was only natural I developed a love for hunting forest whitetails with firearms. It was also only natural that those early gun hunts eventually steered my time and energy toward bowhunting those same forests.

Although bowhunting the big woods remains a tough task, much more information is available now than was available in the late 1960s and early 1970s. Just consider the many specialty magazines now dedicated to hunting white-tailed deer. Printed materials provide hunters a mountain of information. On top of that pile rests nonstop TV shows, hundreds of videos, and countless Web sites geared toward deer hunting. Little of that information was available when every bowhunter toted a recurve and Port Orford cedar shafts into the forests.

As a result, I learned big-woods bowhunting mostly by trial and error. That self-taught bowhunting education, however, played a huge role in my eventual work as a deer hunting educator. With no practical guidelines to follow, I plunged ahead with what I thought were the best options available. I can't tell you how many of my most thoughtful and insightful strategies ended up

36

The author believes his fascination with forests and big woods channeled his energies toward bowhunting these sprawling habitats. Even though he first hunted these areas with a rifle, and still hunts with firearms, he thinks bowhunting is the ultimate big-woods challenge.

Bowhunting success in the deep woods didn't come overnight for the author. Several years passed before he could consistently piece together big-woods puzzles. That didn't happen until the late 1970s, when he had about a decade's worth of experience in his favorite areas.

miles off the mark! Even so, I seldom repeated a mistake.

Sometime around the late '70s I started piecing together much of the forest and deep-woods puzzle. That's also about the time I began tagging big-woods trophies more consistently. As you might imagine, it was difficult to keep those successes a secret from nearby bowhunters. Then again, that was mostly my fault. I couldn't stop running my mouth about those feelings of accomplishment every time I arrowed a trophy whitetail. In addition, I was almost desperate to find one or two dedicated bowhunters to further expand my big-woods knowledge.

That task proved difficult. I had an inkling it took a unique person to bowhunt forest whitetails, but not until I started searching for bowhunting partners did I discover just how rare a breed I was seeking. For about five years I shared my hunting cabin – usually briefly — and my accumulating big-woods knowledge with several individuals. Aside from my brother Jeff, none of those partners had what it took. I finally realized not every bowhunter desires this particular challenge. Not only are forests and deep woods intimidating, they can be downright selfish about letting you see deer. And in many cases, food sources are subtle to invisible to inexperienced eyes. Not only that, but ever-changing natural food choices can cause forest deer to move about the landscape as if they're nomads.

All of my potential hunting partners spent years bowhunting whitetails in farmland habitat. As a result, they were accustomed to quickly identifying food sources and likely deer hangouts. More often than not, forests are a different story. Therefore, new-comers often get out of their truck, look at the seemingly endless forest, scratch their heads and ask: "Where do I start?"

OVERNIGHT SUCCESS?

I can't overstate how much hard work and dedication are required for consistent success on the forest's mature bucks. This remains true even with today's instant access to volumes of helpful deer hunting information. Like it or not, forests offer no shortcuts for applying your book learning to actual hunting situations.

That's why aspiring deep-woods bowhunters should start with a five-year plan. I'm not joking. In fact, five years should be considered a crash course in forest bowhunting. I would wager the average bowhunter will spend seven to eight years bowhunting a particular chunk of forest before he can say he's starting to figure it out. Some readers, I'm sure, don't believe it will take them that long to consistently bow-kill big-woods trophies. I shared that naïve notion during my early years of forest bowhunting. Luckily, I lost that arrogance fast!

The main reason you shouldn't expect instant results is because deep-woods whitetails often change their patterns one season to the next. The No. 1 reason forest bucks sometimes abruptly forsake one area for another — sometimes a great distance away — is the availability and location of preferred foods. It's possible for an area to be overrun with deer and big-buck activity one year but then see few deer and sparse activity the next.

Learning to recognize those changes and react intelligently takes more than one or two deer seasons. Why? I don't know anyone who can spend several months during the off-season walking and studying the big woods. As a result, most of us need several years just learning how to stay on top of things when the whitetail's feeding preferences shift. Further, don't expect such knowledge to accumulate easily. More often than not, the learning curve is taxing and frustrating, and even requires some luck with a heavy dose of persistence.

Realize, too, that my use of the term "five-year plan" is only a point of reference. That's the average amount of time most bowhunters will require to become adept at deciphering deer in these oversized habitats. Some bowhunters will master the art in less time, and some might never master it. Believe me, not everyone will be a five-year success story! I don't say that to demean anyone. I know some excellent bowhunters who just don't want to deal with low numbers of deer sightings, and refuse to tear themselves away from woodlots with high deer densities. That just tells me some people are meant to bowhunt the deep woods and some are meant to bowhunt farmland environments. Of course, a few individuals like me are passionate about bowhunting both environments.

ADOPT THE PROPER PERSPECTIVE

I realize it's one thing to talk about a five-year plan and quite

The author often talks of a "five-year plan" for hunting new areas in a forest, but concedes that's an optimistic time frame. He thinks the average deer hunter must usually spend seven or eight years chasing the big-woods dream before thinking they're close to figuring it out.

another to see it through. Days upon days of deerless hunts and consecutive seasons of unfilled tags can drain the optimism from even the most well-disciplined minds. All of us need occasional success to keep our batteries charged.

This subject often makes me empathize and commiserate with other bowhunters. That's because I often struggled to maintain my optimism when I first started bowhunting. I'll never forget the frustration, hopelessness and failures I experienced during my early big-woods bowhunts. Unfortunately, I let those frustrations overflow into my personal life. It wasn't until a good friend took me aside and pointed out my bad behavior that I even realized what a grouch I had become. I instantly swore that, even though whitetails might be the grandest animal walking the planet, I would not let them dictate my moods.

My highest hurdle was dealing with the many huge bucks taken each year by gun hunters in my favorite hunting areas. That's because I held the selfish notion that I somehow held title to several of those big bucks. After all, I had invested countless hours scouting those bucks during the post-season and throughout spring, and then I hunted them hard during deer season. Seeing someone else shoot them brought more frustration than I could handle. I had to learn deer hunting wasn't about entitlements. People could indeed spend little or no time scouting, and still be just as entitled as me to one of those monster bucks. Though the names and faces of those successful gun hunters were often different, their stories were usually similar. They walked into the woods on opening morning, took a stand at a likely looking spot and shot a big buck. No fuss, no muss, and certainly no scouting!

That seemed unfair, and so I needed a few seasons to overcome my ill will toward other hunters. Again, I received sound advice from a good friend, but knew it was up to me to combat this negativity. I started by reminding myself that besides being a diehard bowhunter I also was an avid gun hunter. Wisconsin allows deer hunters to take two bucks each year, one by bow and one by gun. Although I hunted fairly hard, I had to admit I was using the nine-day gun season more to explore new areas for bowhunting.

I also forced myself to go look at some of the monster bucks shot by gun hunters. My reasons were threefold. First, I wanted to see if I would recognize any of the bucks from my bowhunts. Second, I wanted to hear the stories of how, when and where the bucks were taken. And third, I wanted to take photos of the bucks.

One thing became apparent during my running census of dead bucks. Although some tremendous bucks were shot, one heck of a bunch more survived the gun seasons. That aspect of the big-woods challenge really intrigued me. What did big bucks do during that nine-day gun season to survive? I became so busy talking with hunters, taking photos, cataloging information and

The location and changing availability of preferred foods is the No. 1 reason big-woods bucks abruptly vacate an area and take up residency elsewhere.

43

The author admits to once holding the selfish notion that he "owned" many big bucks killed nearby during the annual firearms season. So deep was his irritation that he couldn't bring himself to visit neighboring deer camps to admire bucks they killed.

scouting new territory that I didn't have time to be depressed during or after gun season. As a bonus, I met quality people along the way. There's always room for new friends in deer hunting.

STAY UPBEAT DURING THE HUNT

One big complaint from my many short-lived bowhunting partners was their many deerless days. As one said, "I don't care if it's bucks, does or fawns, I want to see deer every time I go bowhunting." I told him I understood. What else could I say? Others said they couldn't understand how I kept going back to the forest. I tried to explain the grand scheme of big-woods bowhunting, but to no avail. They refused to see my logic that each deerless day put them that much closer to a productive day—if they paid attention.

It's true that, for the most part, deer densities are much lower in deep-forest environments than they are in farm country. It's also true that forest deer have a heckuva lot more cover for hiding and disguising their movements. Rather than look at such negatives, I dwell on the positives, which are more common than some bowhunters realize. For instance, low deer densities almost always ensure a tight doe-to-buck ratio and good numbers of mature bucks. I've used those facts repeatedly over the years to deal with long days of zero deer sightings. I just know there's a good chance that when I see a deer, it will be wearing antlers. And if it has antlers, there's a good chance it will be a shooter.

There's another positive to low deer densities: more intense competition by bucks for breeding rights. That opens a realm of possibilities for hunting strategies. For instance, as I discovered in my early bowhunts, rattling and calling can be very effective. The same applies to hunting along rub and/or scrape lines.

Earlier I mentioned that the location and availability of choice foods is the most influential factor in the whereabouts of big-woods deer. Concentrated natural food sources—and I don't mean bait piles—are often rare in these environments. Therefore, when you find one, you can bet every nearby deer will key on the spot. That's likely the biggest reason I developed such an exhausting off-season scouting emphasis years ago. Because I spend so much time scouting, I know before each hunt where whitetails will most likely hang out every day of the bow season.

45

Many of the author's early big-woods bowhunting partners grew up hunting farmland bucks in habitats holding many more deer. They didn't last long in the forest. They couldn't understand how anyone could tolerate all those deerless days common to hunting forests.

And because I believe I'm somewhere in the ballpark, there's a chance I'll eventually get a crack at a mature buck. This deeply held belief keeps me going through some tough periods.

I use another critical factor to keep my spirits up: I usually have the forest to myself. I seldom worry about bumping into other bowhunters, and that's a very positive factor! I work my tail off each year to learn the whereabouts of several bucks. Anyone who has done that knows success often hinges on keeping your presence a secret from these bucks. I have confidence I'll pull it off.

However, I can't control how another bowhunter might approach the situation if he stumbles into it. Will he be as concerned as I am with hygiene? Will he be as careful as I am about where he walks when he enters and exits the woods? And will he pay as much attention to the wind and use his scouting information as wisely as I would? Trying to get a mature buck within bow range is a tough task when it's a one-on-one situation. Adding another bowhunter — or more — into the mix turns that tough task into a virtual impossibility.

SUMMARY

One doesn't need to do much digging to find a slew of reasons to not bowhunt forest and deep-woods bucks. And to be honest, I offered only a handful of reasons why anyone should consider trying it. But those few positives far outweigh the many negatives. Keep that in mind the first time you scout a new chunk of forest. The only way your bowhunt will succeed is if you have the proper positive attitude. In fact, your attitude might be the most important thing you take along as you develop into an effective deep-woods predator. And that ain't no jive!

One reason the author enjoys hunting forests and deep woods is this big perk: He seldom worries about bumping into other hunters, especially during the archery season.

CHAPTER FOUR

BREAKING IT DOWN

Unless you've grown up hunting and scouting forests and sprawling woods, these habitats can be intimidating. Unlike farm country, most big woods aren't laid out in neatly defined square-mile chunks. As one of my mentors told me: "Learn the exact lay of the land in the areas you'll hunt and learn to navigate those areas. Otherwise you're better off carrying a few candy bars, a blanket and matches instead of your bow, 'cause it's going to be a while before you step back onto a road again."

I received that advice more than 30 years ago. That's when "big woods" meant just that. The woods I hunted for whitetails were big—really big! The few logging trails dissecting those forests were cut during World War II, and most had been reclaimed by briars and forearm-sized poplars. Few could be traveled with two-wheel-drive cars or trucks, and only a handful of people I knew owned 4x4s.

The forests I bowhunted underwent a dramatic face lift in the late 1970s and through the 1980s when logging resumed in the region. Chunks of cover from 40 acres to entire sections fell to the loggers' saws. I had several rude awakenings when returning to a favorite hunting area and finding it reduced to stumpage. At first I detested the aggressive logging that flattened thousands of acres of my bowhunting areas in northwestern Wisconsin. Within a couple of years, however, I realized the benefits and importance of logging. Deer numbers increased as the forests regenerated with lush growth. The logging also broke the forest into more huntable pieces of property by cutting large blocks of cover down to size.

Even so, these blocks of mixed-age forest covered substantial chunks of land. And thanks to modern logging and road-building practices, Wisconsin's North Woods contained logging trails

When tracking a big buck through a snowy forest in December, the author noticed that the buck seldom used traditional deer travel routes. Not only did it seldom use well-defined trails, it also detoured around long-vacant permanent tree stands.

49

When the author began hunting forests and deep woods in the late 1960s and early '70s, few hunters were using four-wheel-drive trucks, and no one had yet heard of ATVs.

not much lower in quality than some town roads. That put more country in reach of 4x4s and ATVs.

THE INITIAL BREAK-DOWN

I mention logging because if you spend a few years hunting forests and deep woods, it's almost inevitable you'll experience logging activity where you hunt. I view it as a double-edged sword. Logging brings disruption and destruction, but it also brings regeneration and easier access. By creating more-manageable hunting areas, logging reduces the work needed for those first few steps of your five-year plan. As with any large project, never forget that your five-year plan is a process. Each step leads to the next, and you can't complete the entire job

50

Mark your maps and aerial photos with the exact location of logged areas, and the trails and roads loggers use to move equipment and haul their product from the woods. Also pencil in trails that aren't quite where they're shown on maps.

overnight. Commit yourself to thinking long-term, realizing the more carefully you approach these early steps, the better off you'll be five years from now.

This almost goes without saying, but among your first steps is a careful study of topographic maps and up-to-date aerial photos. With few exceptions, logging will not change contour lines! Saddles, funnels, ridgelines, bogs, swamps and creek bottoms will always remain, whether they hold saplings or mature trees. However, if you're looking at 20-year-old aerial photos, don't expect many similarities in the cover when you make the on-site inspection. Also be sure you know what you're looking for on maps and photos, and that you can identify what you're viewing. It might be worth visiting a forester to decipher which tree

Almost all forests and big woods have experienced logging activity in recent years. That's not a complaint, either. A patchwork of logged areas produces great habitat for white-tailed deer.

species can be identified by canopy colors in the photos. These things aren't as obvious as you might think, because different films are used for different aerial photos, depending on the photos' main purpose. On topo maps, learn to identify which terrain features and elevation changes might warrant an up-close look.

Also be careful not to take on more country than you can explore each season. In your early forays into a new area, break up the big woods into bite-size pieces, and then vow to expand your "work area" every year with deeper scouting and hunting probes. You must wear down some shoe leather to verify and take advantage of what you find on those topo maps and aerial photos.

But maybe I'm getting ahead of myself. Let's back up a bit.

After finding some intriguing areas with your topo maps and aerial photos, your next step is to drive around the region to learn more about these sites. There's nothing more humbling than thinking you've found an untouched hunting area after hours of scouting, and then realizing 100 yards beyond your

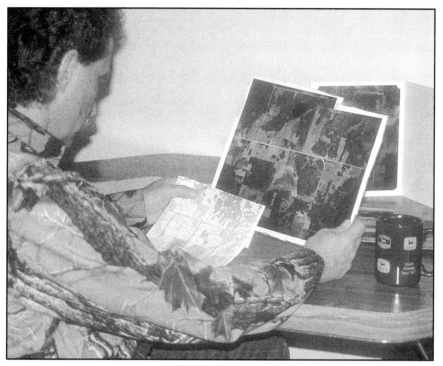

Always study topographic maps and aerial photos of areas you plan to hunt. Whenever possible, scout likely areas exhaustively before bowhunting them.

hotspot is a new road or trail not shown on your 5-year-old maps and photos. A thorough drive "around the block" is especially important as logging activities and new homes spread across North America. Plus, recent logging usually creates deer habitat and more deer, so it's always good to know where these pockets sprout up.

As you drive the roads, pencil in all updates on your topo maps and aerial photos. Mark the exact location of new logging activities and trails the loggers used to haul logs and equipment around the woods. Also double-check the location of older logging sites and their trails in relation to where they're shown on topo maps. I can't tell you how many times I've found my maps to be inaccurate. Things like forest openings, swampy areas and significant changes in elevation sometimes aren't where maps claim.

Another reason to drive roads bordering potential hunting

One drive around a block of forest country and you'll be able to update your topo maps and aerial photos, and discover other people's new land purchases, deer camps and buildings.

areas is to scout for the presence of other hunters. During the late 1900s, many forests and rural regions experienced a mass influx of permanent and seasonal dwellers. Some are hunters who purchased land from paper companies or other large corporations. Those purchases might cover 40 to 640 acres. Yep, entire sections still get bought by some well-heeled folks.

Whatever the property's size, the first thing many new landowners do is build a dwelling, which range from one-room shacks to ultra-modern cabins. Hold it. I take that back. The first thing most of them do is post "No Trespassing" signs on the property's perimeter. Mark these changes in property ownership and access rights on your maps and photos.

By the time you finish your road trips, you'll have a much better feel for which areas to remove from your scouting list, and which areas deserve on-foot reconnaissance. As you can see, this was the first critical step in breaking down the big woods into huntable pieces.

THE INTERNAL BREAK-DOWN

Now it's time to break down your potential hunting sites from

The post-season is perhaps the best time for in-depth scouting expeditions. The author found these rubs while on a North Woods coyote hunt.

the inside. Most aspiring big-timber bowhunters believe this will be relatively easy. I often hear comments like this: "Greg, I spent the entire season bowhunting a forest in my home state. But even with all the time I spent in there, I still feel like a big-woods novice."

They shouldn't sound so surprised. They feel like a novice because that's what they are after only one season! You won't qualify as a big-woods bowhunter until you've stuck with it and paid your dues for several years. And paying those dues means extensive on-foot, on-the-ground, in-the-woods scouting year after year.

I recall an experience 20 years ago that illustrates what is often required. In those days I made my living by finishing concrete, which is a seasonal job in Wisconsin, usually starting in April and ending in November. Anyone who has worked in construction knows it requires many daylight-to-dark work days during those months. Therefore, when I wasn't working, I made the most of it.

The day after Christmas one year, my brother Jeff met me at my cabin in northwestern Wisconsin. We intended to spend at least five days learning the land in several forested areas we had targeted for future hunts. We ended up spending seven full days tramping the woods dawn till dark. Man, did we learn a lot! We were helped tremendously by a blanket of fresh snow about 6 inches deep. Even more importantly, the snow meant we didn't worry much about losing our way, even though this was long before the advent of hand-held GPS units. We knew we could just follow our tracks backward and we'd be OK.

We spent the first few days and evenings studying aerial photos and topo maps, and then walking targeted areas. We walked and walked — and then walked and walked some more. I can't estimate how many miles we logged, but it was a whole bunch! For the most part the deer were in a post-rut pattern. That meant the bucks pretty much were back in their autumn core areas. And thanks to a relatively mild winter to that point, they were going about their business as if it were mid-October. We couldn't have asked for a better situation.

One thing became clear: Even though whitetails had thousands of acres to roam, they pretty much restricted their travels to relatively small areas. And judging by their rubs, the big bucks had used only small parts of the forest during the rut. That was, without doubt, one of the most vital discoveries resulting from our North Woods treks. As we confirmed in the seasons that followed, successful big-woods bowhunting is as much about identifying and "discarding" unproductive country as it is pinpointing and hunting good country. We often walked great distances between pockets of deer sign or sites where we jumped deer from their bedding areas. These big-woods deer didn't bed just anywhere. They chose specific and, surprisingly, very small areas.

On the fourth day of our scouting excursion I got a chance to track a huge buck as it went about its business. That all-day expedition left me with a newfound respect for my big-woods quarry. One thing that stood out most was that the buck didn't repeat the same route once during the next three days. I also noticed this buck seldom followed a well-defined runway or visited food sources every other deer seemed to use. It seemed content to fill its belly with browse foods it found along its route.

My notes from that day helped me recall the buck often made

Consistent success on big-woods bowhunts is as much a matter of recognizing and "discarding" unproductive country as it is pinpointing and hunting productive country.

sudden detours around specific spots. Not until the third occurrence could I interpret the behavior. That's when I stopped and scanned the woods ahead, rather than blindly following the big buck's tracks and unexpected turn. While making my third or fourth scan of the woods ahead, I spotted a permanent tree stand. The platform was about 12 feet off the ground in a triple-trunked maple tree. Two things were obvious: First, the structure had been hastily built. Second, the buck knew it was there. Follow-up scouting trips revealed that other permanent—and illegal, because it's public land—tree stands explained the other route deviations.

Even with that seven-day scouting excursion, Jeff and I only became fairly familiar with two of our targeted areas and slightly familiar with another. We needed several more all-day walks in early spring before feeling we had a handle on things. I often repeat that story because I don't think our experience is the

Many guys want to become big-woods bowhunters and become proficient at taking mature bucks. Few of them, however, devote the time and effort required to achieve this goal because it means forsaking other hobbies during the off-season.

58

exception. Serious, consistent big-woods bowhunting requires everyone to log many hours afoot to have any clue where best to set up on these secretive deer.

AN ALTERNATIVE APPROACH

I realize few bowhunters have the luxury of spending seven straight off-season days to scout a new hunting area. That does-n't mean they'll never arrow a mature buck in the forest or deep woods. It just means they must be wise about using their limited time. Besides family and career, what's most important to you? I've talked with enough bowhunters to know the common answer. Though nearly everyone wants to shoot a big-woods buck, few devote the time and effort to achieve that goal. They have other priorities.

In my case, I put aside other hobbies to achieve the goal. I gave up ice fishing, spring fishing and predator hunting — which was a big love. That gave me more time to walk and learn more about my chosen areas. For me, the rewards outweighed the sacrifices. For other people, they don't. To each his own.

Remember, too, that almost everyone is within realistic driving distance of a forest or big woods. In most cases these places can be reached all winter. If you're serious about it, you'll need only a few weekends of diligent scouting to develop a basic understanding of an area. A few weekends more should provide intimate understanding.

SUMMARY

From that point forward, because you'll know what to look for, you'll realize it's now easier to break down new big-woods areas. Always keep in mind, however, to start small and then work your way outward into surrounding areas. You're far better off knowing one area intimately than being vaguely familiar with several.

And never forget the five-year plan. Until you start bowhunting these areas and adapting your hunts to what the deer are doing, you won't really know how the pieces come together. Don't become impatient. The more carefully you learn the details of your hunting area, the more successful you'll be in the years ahead.

59

CHAPTER FIVE

THE CURSE OF QUICK SUCCESS

Even though my passion for chasing whitetails in forests and deep woods was instilled at a young age, I can assure you it didn't result from beginner's luck! My family's big-woods background had more to do with it. My father, grandfather, a couple of uncles, a few cousins and some of their friends got that ball rolling in the early 1940s. Each of these gentlemen had more than 20 years of big-woods deer hunting experience by the time I joined them on their annual treks to the North Woods.

I shot my first big-woods whitetail, a doe, during one of those early hunts, but several seasons passed before I again tasted success. Long waits between kills might dim some hunters' views of big-woods deer hunting, but that didn't happen to me. Before I ever hunted those forests, I knew quick success seldom translated into consistent success. After all, I had seen the low success rates of my dad and his hunting partners for too many years to assume I could shoot a deer every gun season. Therefore, I knew the challenge would only increase when I tried ambushing forest bucks with a bow and arrow.

That isn't to say, however, that I've never fallen victim to the curse of quick success when hunting a new area since then. I have, but I learned not to read too much into each quick success. To stay grounded in reality, I just recall my early big-woods hunts and remind myself that I'll never totally figure out trophy whitetails.

WHY QUICK SUCCESS IS A CURSE

Of course, I had some lapses along the way. But as soon as I started thinking I had these deep-woods monarchs figured out—

60

The author learned at an early age that quick success, or beginner's luck, seldom translates into consistent success over the long haul. Nowhere is this more true than when bowhunting forests and deep woods.

Many bowhunters believe the strategies they used to waylay one big buck will work in any situation in the years that follow. It might work again, but don't count on it.

62

and talked smart about it — they taught me otherwise. I soon conceded that no human can ever totally figure out mature white-tailed bucks, no matter where they might live!

Not everyone agrees, though. I remember a conversation in the mid-1990s with a hunter who enjoyed a massive dose of quick success: He arrowed a Boone and Crockett buck during his first bowhunt in northern Wisconsin's forests. As I remember, his boast went something like this: "Big-woods hunting isn't all that tough. I think I'll be able to shoot a big buck almost every year."

As I write this book, about 10 years have passed since that conversation and, as you might assume, that lucky hunter hasn't enjoyed one successful hunt since. Further, it's not as if he's passing up smaller bucks in hopes of shooting another monster. He's had a tough time laying eyes on even borderline shooters.

When I talked to him in those intervening years, it seemed obvious he was cursed by his quick success. Killing that monster buck made him think he could hunt the same area with the same strategies every season. He saw no need for further scouting, and made no attempt to broaden his big-woods bowhunting horizons. He truly believed he had figured out this trophy whitetail thing.

Unfortunately, that false sense of security isn't unique to him. Every year I meet hunters who walked into the woods the previous fall, shot a big deer, and dragged it out of the woods believing they had found the forest's honey hole. Hey, if one big buck was in that area, there must be others, right? Why waste precious time and energy searching elsewhere when you're dialed into the best site? Obviously, they'd rather spend their time reliving the hunt and flashing photos of their trophy to everyone they meet.

In my experience, each forest has darned few areas that produce monster bucks year after year. That's because forests and big woods are living entities. They might not look like they're changing every year, and you might even overlook the changes if you wait five years between visits, but trust me, forests are never static environments. As habitats change, so does the behavior of deer using them. You can take that to the bank!

LEARNING THE HARD WAY

Perhaps I preach so much about the curse of quick success because I hate to see hunters make the same mistakes I've made!

In fact, I let it trap me twice in a five-year span. The first instance involved a big buck I chased for much of one autumn. I had seen the trophy several times in broad daylight during mid-October, unusual for most big-woods hunts. Thanks to those sightings and some reconnaissance work, I pinpointed a couple of his primary travel routes. Even so, we played cat-and-mouse for a couple of weeks before everything fell into place. I finally closed the deal on a snappy-cold November morning.

I remember standing over that buck and thinking I had figured out big-woods deer hunting. Little did I know just how much more I needed to learn about consistently taking the forest's mature bucks. The next three seasons passed without success, which should have told me something. But after I killed a buck during the fourth autumn that followed, I again overrated my abilities. I sank even deeper into overconfidence when I arrowed another trophy the next season.

One reason I overestimated myself was that the first of those bucks, a big-bodied 8-pointer, was a testament to relentless pursuit and the perfect execution of a new, highly effective big-woods strategy. I first located the buck while scouting in late August. I was walking down an old logging trail early in the morning when I spotted him drinking from a puddle in the trail. He didn't notice me for nearly 30 seconds, which gave me time to study the velvet-antlered brute.

I became obsessed with that buck, and I hunted him hard, but smartly. It probably helped that my construction job limited my free time to weekends. Also, I hunted him only when conditions were perfect. On some weekends I invaded his turf two or three times, but then I'd leave him alone other weekends. I arrowed him Nov. 2, which meant my pursuit of that buck lasted six weeks.

That was 1980, and I was using a new strategy that eventually became my trademark: I had set up along his rub lines. That strategy, coupled with the fact I had actually killed a buck I targeted, convinced me I had mastered big-woods bowhunting. My confidence was bolstered the next season when I again used my new rub-line strategy to kill another big-woods trophy. That success came in late October, which is peak pre-rut time in the forest I was hunting. Unbelievably, the 10-pointer I arrowed was the sixth buck to walk past me on that rub line in a 10-minute span.

Contrary to what some bowhunters believe, darned few areas in a big woods will produce monster bucks year after year. Forests and big woods are living entities and are changing every year. As habitats change, so does the behavior of deer using them.

Those two memorable archery seasons of 1980 and '81, however, didn't start a long string of bigger and better bowhunts. Although I had several close calls the next three seasons, I came home empty-handed. That's when I realized I had again let myself be victimized by my previous success. Yes, I had pieced together a new strategy for hunting big-woods whitetails, and it helped me shoot mature bucks in consecutive years. The fact remained, however, that I got my butt kicked the next three seasons. Obviously, my strategy required more study and fine-tuning. That's about the time my brother, Jeff, and I started hitting our big-woods hunting areas more often during the off-season. I can't believe how beneficial those intense scouting and shed-antler hunting missions proved to be.

THINGS TO SEEK

For one thing, off-season scouting trips often dispel misconceptions. Hunters who experience quick success in forests and deep woods often don't know for sure why big bucks they killed were in a certain area. They often assume the bucks were drawn there by antlerless deer, and that guess is often correct. After all, big bucks often lurk where antlerless deer hang out — at all times of the year.

OK, but why were the antlerless deer in that area? Experienced big-woods bowhunters know the important role that food plays in the whitetail's everyday routines. Further, these guys know their success hinges on their ability to pinpoint the deer's most desirable foods. Even more importantly, experienced hunters know that the feeding preferences of big-woods whitetails can change overnight.

When one site goes cold, can you predict feeding sites where deer likely moved? To stay atop the action you must get off your duff and go scouting. Even more importantly, you must know what you're seeking. Don't assume you'll just know it when you find it. First and foremost, realize natural-growing browse provides the main food source for big-woods whitetails. To narrow it further, whitetails prefer the most tender — that is, youngest — browse foods they can find.

Just about every big woods I've hunted had recent and/or current logging activity — or in some cases — a major fire, wind

One of the author's most memorable hunts involved an 8-point buck that made him obsessive. To the author's credit, he hunted the buck hard, but also carefully and intelligently.

By the early 1980s, the author was developing a bowhunting strategy that was effective for big-woods bucks. He had learned to piece together active rub lines and then find strategic spots along the routes to hang his tree stands.

storm or insect infestation that created a temporary hole in the habitat. Hey folks, all those "catastrophes" might look like giant scars on the landscape, but they quickly regenerate into abundant browse foods for whitetails. There's an old saying that whitetails follow the ax and the blaze. Depending on the acreage involved, these areas can become deer magnets for years!

Personally, I like to concentrate on smaller logged areas, ideally, no more than 40 acres. Because small sites are quickly scouted, it doesn't take long to figure out whether deer are using these small sites, and where exactly their feeding activities are concentrated. Several years ago, Jeff and I spent almost an entire season bowhunting one 80-acre clearcut. I can't remember one hunt when each of us didn't see at least a dozen deer. We saw does, fawns, small bucks, medium-sized bucks and huge bucks. These sightings were consistent from opening weekend through the rut. Both of us had several tree stands near the cut, which allowed us to hunt there no matter what the wind conditions. We also took pains to silently slip into and out of our hunting spots.

IN-SEASON SCOUTING

The forest won't reveal all of its food sources during the off-season, however. To keep tabs on mast crops and other foods that drop within reach of hungry mouths, you must scout during the season. Just be sure to take the low-impact approach. When I scout during the season, I walk into a targeted area, take a quick look, pick several potential stand sites, and get out. The less time you spend in an area, and the less wandering around you do, the better. You must not give whitetails a heads-up before you hang a tree stand.

Always monitor acorns because when they're available, little else matters to the whitetail's stomach. Acorns attract and hold whitetails within small areas. Be forewarned, however, that oaks are rare to nonexistent in some Northern big woods. That's why I consider them an "occasional" food source. Again, the key to locating oak stands is to do some legwork. Unlike logging, fires and other disruptions to the landscape, acorn-bearing oaks can be a challenge to locate. I've hunted areas where stands of mature oaks were so well-hidden that it was like searching for the proverbial needle in a haystack.

Before you start walking daylight till dark in search of oaks, or specific species of oaks, visit a local forester or logger who knows something about the region's trees. These individuals usually know the exact location of every oak stand in the county, which saves lots of legwork. When visiting these experts, make sure you're marking your map or aerial photo!

Again, pay attention to smaller stands of oaks so you can figure out quickly where to place your stands. In addition, small stands are often overlooked by other hunters, so you won't have to worry about competition. When acorns rain onto the forest floor, experienced bowhunters design their hunts around them. Most bowhunters, however, gravitate to larger, more obvious oak stands, even though it's akin to setting up on a 320-acre beanfield. Especially when acorns are abundant, deer could pop out anywhere and feed forever in one area, never offering a bow shot.

Not only that, but if the stand is well-known by other bowhunters, don't be surprised if all you see are females and younger bucks. Trying to kill a mature big-woods buck is tough enough when it's just you and the buck. That task borders on the impossible when other hunters are making the same chase!

LEARN WHAT THEY EAT

I often hear big-woods hunters complain that it's tough to pinpoint where deer are feeding. One guy told me, "I don't think the deer in my area concentrate on any one spot. There's just too much food out there."

I've hunted big-woods whitetails in many regions and habitat types. I have yet to see an instance where the deer didn't concentrate their feeding activities to some degree on a particular food. In some instances I couldn't name which buds, grasses, twig tips or ground-hugging plant they were eating, but I learned to identify the food at a glance. I learned long ago that nothing is more conclusive than watching a deer eat, and whitetails existing on natural forage eat constantly. Always watch closely when does and fawns walk by, and let them show you which foods they want. Nothing is more conclusive. This helps you zero in on which oaks are producing the best acorns, which dead-falls provide the tastiest buds or lichens, or which part of a clearcut grows the most succulent browse. Then it's just a matter of fine-tuning stand sites.

Always strive to figure out what deer are eating in forests and big woods. When they feed on new growth sprouting up in clearcuts, try to figure out which species of young trees they prefer, and where deer find them in abundance

The author puts a lot of stock in watching what deer eat when they're browsing their way down a trail. Nothing is more conclusive in determining food preferences than seeing what goes into their mouths.

SUMMARY

Sadly, hunters who become victims of their own success have no idea what they're missing, and that's especially true in big-woods settings. When you consider how some bowhunters consciously forsake thousands of acres of forests by limiting themselves to a sliver of land, you better understand the powerful influence of quick success. It casts a spell some hunters never escape.

Then again, this is a lesson they must learn on their own. If they don't try to break the spell, they only hurt themselves while benefiting you and me. Those of us who explore our own failures and learn from our mistakes enjoy more consistent success. Each time you succeed, approach the next season as if it's your first. Force yourself to break out of your ruts and take a more aggressive approach to bowhunting big-woods bucks.

If the forests or big woods where you bowhunt have oaks, you're best off concentrating your efforts on smaller stands of oaks. These smaller parcels are less likely to be noticed by other hunters.

73

CHAPTER SIX

TERRAIN AND COVER: KEYS TO SUCCESS

Even though I spent more time looking at my dad's back than I did studying the North Woods around us during my first hunts, I managed to get a decent orientation into hunting deep-woods whitetails as a youth. If nothing else, I became familiar with the location and general lay of main roads and logging trails.

Those hunts formed the basis for much of my first 10 to 15 years of bowhunting forests and the deep woods. Starting in the late 1980s, though, I broadened my big-woods bowhunting horizons by exploring other forested regions in Wisconsin, Minnesota, Michigan, Manitoba, Alberta and Saskatchewan.

As I hunted each region, I quickly realized each big-woods environment had its own unique terrain and cover characteristics. In some cases the differences were subtle, but in others I felt as if I had entered a new world of big-woods bowhunting. Some of these habitats are flat, swampy and almost impenetrably thick. Others are dry, hilly and somewhat open. I've also bowhunted deep-woods habitats that feature almost equal amounts of hills, swamps, thick brush and open stands of mature timber.

But no matter what the terrain and cover, one constant remains: To achieve consistent success, you must learn how whitetails use their surroundings and why. How do these deer relate to the terrain and cover, and how do their routines change, depending on weather, food and season?

Before you can hope for consistent success as a forest bowhunter, you must learn how the area's whitetails use their surroundings for resting, feeding and traveling.

Saddles, ridgetops, ridgelines, intersecting ridges, creek bottoms and other distinct terrain features are important keys to defining and concentrating the whitetail's travel corridors. And when you mix in good edge cover with these breaks, even better hunting sites stand out as you scout. Realize, too, that edge situations exist in many places other than where expanses of open ground border large blocks of cover.

DIFFERENT TERRAIN REQUIRES DIFFERENT SCOUTING

As I began venturing into other forests in my travels, I discovered just how good northwestern Wisconsin had been to me! The area I bowhunted for many years, though expansive, wasn't difficult to break down and decipher. My home forests feature a good mix of low, swampy ground and fairly pronounced ridges on higher ground. As a result, I could usually figure out where whitetails preferred to walk in those deep woods. They almost always related to some type of an edge, whether along swamp edges, terrain breaks, regrowing cuts, or meandering creek bottoms.

In fact, in many cases I could drive around and locate such spots from forest roads. I also found potential hotspots by studying topo maps and aerial photos. Swamp edges, creek bottoms, large forest openings and recent clearcuts are readily identifiable on up-to-date maps and photos. That story ended when I shifted my attention outside my home state. Unlike northwestern Wisconsin's obvious terrain and cover features, the forests and deep woods I branched into were mostly featureless — at least at first glance from a distance. These "new" forests and big woods required my up-close and personal approach.

Two factors jumped out during my first scouting trips. First, in many cases the elevation was significantly different from what appeared on topo maps. Second, the cover was considerably thicker than what appeared on aerial photos, often reducing visibility to 30 yards and less. What do I consider significant differences? I don't mean 5- to 10-foot differences, which would call into question a map's credibility. No, these differences were more like 2- to 5-foot variances, which are significant for flat, swampy habitat. I mention this because each chunk of subtle "high ground" inside swamps often reveals big-buck sign. In one new area, I found so many rubs on 4- to 8-inch trees that it bor-

The author's brother Jeff arrowed this buck while hunting in Manitoba's Spruce Woods National Forest. This is a great deep-woods area.

dered on ridiculous. The higher ground also attracted tremendous scraping activity. Big bucks keyed on the high ground because antlerless deer were spending lots of time there.

Obviously, the only way to find those big-buck hangouts was to get out of the truck and walk the area. Nothing on my topo maps or aerial photos hinted that those places existed. My hunting partner and I even scoured our aerial photos with a magnifying glass. Try was we might, nothing stood out from its surroundings.

What else do I look for in terms of terrain features? The most

Big-woods whitetails love to hang out near and inside swamps. No matter which forests or deep woods you hunt, check to see if they contain swamps, and then scout them. They provide great cover and easy access to food and water.

As with whitetails in other habitats, big-woods bucks relate to sudden changes and transitions in terrain. And because whitetails are creatures of the edge, look for transitions in cover types, too.

productive big-woods hotspots I've ever bowhunted are swamp edges, especially large swamp edges bordering large stands of oaks, poplar and birch. Therefore, I start by scanning for them on topo maps, but I realize some big-woods regions contain miles of swamp edge! I narrow it down by focusing on those that feature more twists and turns than others. I then narrow my options further by concentrating on swamp edges with the most severe twists and turns.

That particular facet of fine-tuning my scouting efforts came to me after many years of experience. I once thought one swamp edge was pretty much like the next. Then I realized that mature bucks seemed especially fond of swamp edges bordering hardwoods like oak, maple, birch and poplar. Why do big bucks love gnarly swamp edges? I assume these twisting, turning edges provide many places for bucks to scan the country ahead while remaining somewhat hidden. Each time the swamp juts into a hardwood flat, it creates a point of thick cover. With few exceptions, the backside of these points — the direction bucks come from — hold more big-buck sign than any other area along edges. That's probably because big bucks spend lots of time at these spots, alternately rubbing, scraping and scanning the landscape ahead for danger. Only when convinced everything is safe do they walk around the end of the point and continue on their way.

Although it's often possible to locate swamp-edge points on topo maps and aerial photos, my advice from earlier chapters stands: Never rate a site's big-buck potential without on-site scouting and evaluation. Once you complete that task, you're one step closer to setting up your ambush. Back in the mid-1980s, for instance, I arrowed a 10-pointer in northwestern Wisconsin as it eased along a rub line paralleling a tamarack swamp. My tree stand was located where the swamp jutted into a chunk of dry, higher ground. Judging by the buck's relaxed behavior during the 15 minutes before I released my shot, he felt comfortable on that travel route. I'm sure the lay of the land had much to do with it.

I'm often asked why I spend little or no time bowhunting small humps of dry ground inside swamps, especially since they usually hold so much sign. These "swamp islands," as I call them, are virtual deer magnets, but whitetails use them almost exclusively for bedding. Not only that, but for most of the Wisconsin archery season I would have to wade through potentially chest-deep water to reach them. No buck is worth a cold-water dunk far from a friend or truck. Not only that, but in most cases I would have to push through dense cover and make more noise than I prefer. Every deer within earshot would know where to find me, and that's no good! That's why I shy away from swamp islands as stand sites.

RIDGES AND RIDGELINES

Though not as productive as swamp edges, ridgelines offer big-woods whitetails several travel options. As with swamp edges,

Big-woods deer often follow travel routes bordering swamps. This is where you'll often find great concentrations of rubbing and scraping activity.

all ridgelines are not created equal. Look for those with distinct characteristics, and that doesn't mean thick cover. I'm amazed so many deer hunters believe mature bucks, especially forest bucks, always seek dense cover for traveling. I've been hunting and scouting these intense creatures more than a couple of decades, and that just isn't true. Other factors are more vital in guiding their movements.

One critical factor is the terrain itself, especially in rolling, hilly or mountainous terrain. Rather than walking through dense cover, mature bucks prefer to walk where they have a decent view of the woods ahead while being within a bound or two of safety. Notice I said safety, not thick cover. Thick cover isn't the only form of refuge whitetails seek when escaping threats. For instance, they know how to take advantage of narrow hog's-back, or razor-back ridges. Whitetails often walk narrow ridges because one bound in the opposite direction of danger puts the ridgeline between them and the threat.

Big-woods deer use other types of ridgelines for travel, of course. One of their favorite ridgelines, in fact, is the opposite of the easily identified hog's back. I call these flattop ridges "flats," and they usually cover lots of ground. More specifically, they're slightly more than a bowshot across at their widest points. Most flattop ridges have an obvious runway down their middle. However, the less obvious runways on the flat's outside edges almost always draw most big-buck travel. Why? Again, at the slightest hint of danger, they turn, jump over the ridge's edge and disappear.

Though big-woods bucks like to travel ridgeline flats year-round, they especially like them during the rut! That's because these flats let them check lots of ground for hot does while using little energy. Not only can they scan the flats, they can also see much of the hillsides and valleys below.

Ridgeline saddles are another terrain feature to seek and inspect when scouting ridges. Saddles are nothing more than dips or swales in a ridgeline. In the rare event you don't know, whitetails are famous for saving energy by cutting through saddles when crossing ridges. In that regard, they're as predictable as us. We'll also cross ridges at their lowest points, i.e. saddles. When establishing stand sites in saddles, realize that whitetails are wary of ambushes when moving through confined areas,

Mature bucks take advantage of several factors besides dense cover while traveling, and when pausing before entering openings, feeding areas, bedding areas and other parts of their range.

83

By hanging toward the outside edges of ridgetop flats, big bucks are never more than a bound or two from safety.

such as funnels, and saddles and narrow valleys. Take extra care when selecting and preparing these stands, making sure you're downwind and well-concealed.

OTHER HIDDEN EDGES

Besides swamp edges, several other hidden edges can be found in most forests and deep woods. The most common are edges caused by logging, fires, tornadoes, wind storms, insect infestations, beaver impoundments or any other phenomenon

The most productive edges combine relatively abrupt changes in cover and terrain, such as where a heavy forest suddenly ends along a swamp, clearcut or beaver flowage at the foot of a hill or atop a ridge.

Regardless of whether water is present in a lake, pond, river or creek basin, the edges of that feature act as a natural barrier to whitetails.

that flattens or kills a chunk of forest. The most productive hidden edges in such situations are those where the living forest butts up to the site where everything was cut, burned, killed or flattened. Whitetails increasingly gravitate toward these edges as trees and vegetation regrow.

Other less obvious and, hence, difficult edges to locate are those where brush and trees make a sudden, natural transition from thick cover to relatively open terrain. In most instances these hidden edges occur where the forest canopy changes. A thick-canopied mature forest allows less sunlight to hit the ground, which means less underbrush. The opposite occurs where the canopy is younger and not as thick.

Though subtle, these hidden edges are often productive. And, as noted, they can be downright tough to find. Most don't show up on topo maps, and they can be difficult to spot on aerial photos. Finding them entails legwork. As with other types of edges, the more twists and turns present, the more productive they'll be.

Without a doubt, the most important factor in all big-woods habitats is water, because it creates more edges on ponds, creeks, rivers, swamps and lakes than any other natural factor. Whitetails always use these edges as natural barriers, to some degree. One thing I've noticed about hunting near watery edges, however, is that whitetails seem especially suspicious and flighty when near the water itself. No matter if they're drinking, traveling or just hanging out, whitetails are on high alert! Why? I assume deer, and all prey animals, realize water isn't a great deterrence to four-legged predators like wolves, coyotes, bears, bobcats and domestic dogs. Deer, especially, prefer to outrun predators, and swimming dramatically slows their flight and reduces maneuverability.

SUMMARY

I can sum up this chapter with few words: Nothing tells you more about terrain and cover than spending time in those areas. If you're looking for shortcuts to success, this book isn't for you. Even if I could scout with you, I guarantee we would walk several days before I'd confidently select the best possible sites. Therefore, all I guarantee is this: Your success on mature bucks will rise in direct correlation with how well you know the area's terrain and cover. Take it one step at a time, literally!

CHAPTER SEVEN

OF CLEARCUTS, BURNS & WINDSTORM DAMAGE

As with whitetails in other environments, the routines of big-woods deer revolve around two elements: food and cover. Whenever possible, they try to set up shop near their primary feeding areas. Of course, the proximity of suitable cover to those foods dictates how much traveling is required. That's a critical factor to consider when scouting for non-rut bowhunting stand sites.

As the title of this chapter indicates, several factors can suddenly create forest openings. With each new opening comes food and edge cover. One thing to realize, however, is that openings created by fires, logging, windstorms, tree diseases and insect infestations seldom remain open for long. Given sufficient moisture, these openings become choked with dense cover within a few years. Besides becoming a great food source, this dense cover soon provides deer with prime bedding habitat. Although these spots can be difficult to walk through, they act as whitetail havens, which means they can be keys to big-woods bowhunting success.

BURNS & CLEARCUTS

I lump burns and clearcuts together because forest whitetails

Forest openings provide food and edge cover. Remember, though, that these openings seldom remain open for long.

The author will never forget the look of shock and surprise on his father's face when their station wagon rolled into a favorite hunting area. The once-expansive, long-standing poplar forest had disappeared since the previous deer season!

relate to them for similar reasons. Also, effective approaches to bowhunting in and around them are nearly identical.

I remember when, after being absent from our hunting area for years, logging resumed in earnest. I was 14 years old and about to start my second gun-hunting season. The day before the season opened, my dad, brother Mike and I headed out to scout. I'll never forget the shock on Dad's face as our station wagon rolled up to our hunting area. The once-expansive poplar forest that had stood since my dad first hunted this region was gone. In its place was a clearcut. The woods had been logged the previous spring.

Although he was upset initially, Dad regained his composure. He opened the car door, stood on the floorboards, and looked across the clearcut. He studied the area a few moments and then announced we would hunt there anyway. Dad's decision paid huge dividends on opening day when he connected on a beautiful 9-pointer at mid-morning. Mike shot his first deer, a doe, just after daylight. I can't remember how many deer I saw, but it was nearly two dozen, and several of them wore headgear. Only one

Burned areas stay black and desolate only a short time. As new growth sprouts and shoots skyward, wildlife of all kind moves in to take advantage of food and cover in the years that follow.

91

of those bucks, a forkhorn, presented a shot. Unfortunately, in all the excitement, I didn't press my cheek into the stock of my .308, and my bullet whistled harmlessly over the buck's back.

In recalling our experiences, I realize that eventful morning was no accident. Dad knew that, because of the clearcut, the area would be full of whitetails. He also knew the deer would most likely hang out there until first light and then head deeper into the forest, where our stand sites were located.

That incident occurred in the late 1960s, but I remember it as if it were yesterday. I also remember the other 11 members of Dad's gun-hunting camp didn't fare so well that day. But, as was the group's custom, Dad invited them to hunt our honey hole the next day. Several members accepted the invitation, including my uncle Clayton Boese. Clayton nailed a nice 8-pointer at midday, and another group member missed a huge buck.

As logging in that part of northwestern Wisconsin increased the next few years, deer numbers rose along with it. By the time I returned from a four-year stint with the U.S. Air Force in 1974, the deer herd was at an all-time high in my life.

Soon after my return, I saw the magnetic effect forest fires have on deer. In 1975 a fire raged through nearly 100,000 acres of northwestern Wisconsin's deep woods. The western edge of the blaze was just a few miles from our cabin. I remember the terrible sense of loss the first time I drove through the burn, which resembled the lunar surface. No trees, no underbrush, no plants and, as a result, virtually no life. But as I found out, life soon returned in abundance. If memory serves, that fire roared to life in late April and wasn't extinguished until mid-May, so the burned area had all summer to rejuvenate. By the time archery season opened in mid-September, the burn was covered with deer and all sorts of other wildlife.

These incidents are perfect examples of the drawing power that "catastrophic" clearings caused by fires and logging have on whitetails. Interestingly, the way whitetails related to the two clearings was nearly identical. For instance, the first year after the cut or burn little or no woody cover remained. However, an abundance of nutritious deer foods raced to fill the void. Whether it's grasses, weeds, discarded treetops, hardwood shoots, poplar suckers or low brush, whitetails love it! They also

92

Nothing steers a bowhunter's stand selection more accurately and reliably than seeing a big ol' buck using a particular travel corridor.

It's crucial to keep a buffer zone between you and any area that bucks might use as bedding sanctuaries.

love the fact they can fill their bellies with little effort.

In my experience, clearcuts and burned areas are most productive for trophy whitetails during their first year of regrowth. Not only will deer use the areas, but they'll be relatively easy to pattern and hunt. Provided you aren't careless, and provided the area is large enough, you should be able to focus a full season's worth of hunting on one clearcut or burn.

HUNT THE EDGES FIRST

Because first-year burns and clearcuts don't provide ideal bedding cover, whitetails must rest elsewhere in daylight. Although big-woods whitetails commonly travel farther than their farmland cousins, they won't bed any farther from feeding areas than necessary. When I start bowhunting new openings, I establish my bowhunting setups closer to the edge of the burn or clearcut than to the deer's likely bedding areas. In fact, in most cases I pick stand sites bordering the feeding area.

I do that for two reasons. First, in most cases the deer I'm hunting haven't received much, if any, pressure. That means they should be active during daylight. Second, setups near the edge of large openings usually afford excellent views. I can't stress enough the importance of this point.

I can't begin to tell you how many of the big bucks I've arrowed came as a direct result of scouting. In many cases, I never laid eyes on the buck I targeted until moments before I shot. Unlike farm country, where the more-open landscape offers more big-buck sightings, forest habitat seldom grants long-range views. Therefore, bowhunters must interpret sign when trying to pattern big bucks. I like to think my sign-interpretation skills are sharp, but I also know they require speculation and educated guesses about what I observe. As a result, I sometimes end up holding the bag after misinterpreting deer sign.

That's why I advise setting up near the edges of first- and second-year burns and clearcuts. Not only will this position you to ambush deer as they enter (evenings) and leave (mornings) the openings, but it also positions you to watch deer activity in other parts of the clearing. When it comes to situating your stand just right, there's nothing like seeing a big ol' buck using a specific corridor.

In most cases, you can obtain such observations well beyond

The author has learned the hard way that you seldom, if ever, get the drop on a big-woods buck by bowhunting from a hastily prepared ground blind.

the first couple of years of a new burn or clearcut. In fact, as long as you don't overhunt the big buck's travel corridor, it's possible the spot will remain productive for at least a decade. Remember, these regrowing areas offer a smorgasbord of nutritional foods, and evolve into good bedding cover for at least 10 years as saplings and brush take over.

In fact, as deer begin using these sites to bed, it might be time to hunt their interiors. First, thoroughly scout the sites for bedding areas in the off-season, preferably soon after hunting season and again during spring. It's nearly impossible to walk through regrowing burns and clearcuts without making noise, so any deer you spook while scouting will have long forgotten the intrusion by autumn. Scouting missions immediately after the season are often my most beneficial trips. You'll get a fresh view of how whitetails were using the cut. And talk about a great time to pinpoint big-buck bedding areas! Because fall is so far away, I actually try to jump bucks from their beds.

One of the keys to my big-woods success is that I almost always knew where the bucks I killed were bedding. In almost every instance I learned those details while post-season scouting. When armed with such information, I had a much easier time figuring out where to hang my tree stands. When choosing stand sites, I search for pockets of buck sign. Another good bet is to set up near grassy, weedy openings inside the regrowth that attract feeding activity. Also look for dense internal stands of hardwood saplings, which deer love to eat.

When bowhunting within burns and clearcuts, stand options are usually limited. Few trees will be large enough to support a portable stand and hide your outline. Your only option might be hunting from the ground, which gives you two choices: You can build a blind using brush and branches, or use a manufactured pop-up blind. Either way, keep a couple of factors in mind. First, ground blinds must be set up long enough in advance to let deer grow accustomed to them. Second, blinds built from branches, brush and foliage must be elaborate enough to let you draw your bow undetected with deer nearby. Trust me, whitetails won't let you get away with bowhunting from a hastily prepared ground blind.

As burns and clearcuts surpass the 10-year mark, whitetails

97

BOWHUNTING FORESTS & DEEP WOODS

relate to them differently. Although bedding cover usually remains adequate, food availability starts declining, and deer must travel elsewhere to eat. Don't be concerned. We all know whitetails are creatures of habit, and they pass those habits and patterns from one generation to the next. They often continue to use the same travel corridors their predecessors used when the burn or clearcut was a year or two old.

One last thing: If a burn or clearcut covers 100 acres or more, it's possible to bowhunt that one area almost exclusively all season if you never ignore wind direction. Never trust this to luck or fate. If the wind is from the west, concentrate your efforts on the western side of the opening, and so on.

WINDSTORMS

Bowhunting wind-flattened areas is an extremely tough gig. Unlike burns and clearcuts, where much of the felled material was turned to ash or hauled away, trees in wind-flattened areas remain. Worse, they're strewn about in every possible direction. Talk about a jungle! On the plus side, these sites quickly become popular deer hangouts. Again, if the flattened area is 100 acres or more, it will provide almost unlimited deer food.

That factor has positive and negative effects. Although such sites provide nearly unlimited nutritional supplies, deer have no reason to walk outside of these sites. And taking "the fight" to them is usually a futile, frustrating experience. I find it's better to bowhunt these areas by setting up in strategic spots on their perimeters and hoping for some luck. That's what I do when bowhunting first-year windfall areas.

After that, I take a different approach, one that usually takes a year or two to exploit. Because deer have a relatively tough time walking through wind-flattened areas, their movements are restricted. As a result, deer trails soon appear. Even so, it's not a slam-dunk bowhunting setup. After all, wind-fall areas are usually thick and darned near impenetrable. About the only way to quietly navigate is by following deer trails, and anytime we use deer trails for access, we're flirting with disappointment.

SUMMARY

When bowhunting forest openings, never let your guard down.

98

Trying to penetrate and bowhunt the interior of a first-year blown-down area can be a study in frustration.

The main problem with bowhunting blown-down areas is that you usually must use deer trails as walking trails. Therefore, it's almost impossible to hide your presence.

The damage caused by heavy logging equipment often helps create the exact type of habitat that attracts big-woods whitetails.

Practice scent control at all times. But realize, too, that no matter what precautions you take to become "odor-free," if you repeatedly walk on deer trails, you'll be detected eventually. And once a mature buck believes it's being hunted, your chances of seeing him in daylight are pretty much nonexistent. That's why, when it comes to blown-down areas, I suggest bowhunting only occasionally during their first few years. And despite what I said about the difficulties of staying odor-free, you must do your best to eliminate human odor when moving about or hunting these areas. Although you might never eliminate it, the more you reduce your scent, the better your odds of ambushing a mature buck.

CHAPTER EIGHT

IS DEEPER REALLY BETTER?

Darkness was enveloping the forest when I looked at my watch. Legal hunting hours had officially ended. I grabbed the pull-rope, tied it to my bow and slowly lowered it to the ground. I then removed my portable stand from the oak where I had spent the previous three hours.

Once on the ground I double-checked to ensure I wouldn't leave anything behind. Darkness had nearly swallowed up the forest by the time I began the trek toward a distant township road. I took only a few steps before stopping to dig a flashlight from my daypack. The bright glow told me the batteries held a strong charge.

I walked fast for 15 minutes before stopping to rest. Although the forest was now totally dark, I knew my exact location. I had made this hike so many times I swore I could have found my way without the flashlight, but I had no intention of proving my point!

I arrived at my vehicle about 35 minutes after leaving the tree. "That's quite a hike," I whispered to myself. Then, as usual, I reminded myself it was worth the time and energy to pull off that hunt. The monotony of three hours on stand had been broken by a huge male bobcat an hour before dark. The cat had hung around my tree on the oak ridge nearly 15 minutes before picking me off. We locked eyes briefly before the cat beat a retreat into the nearby ash swamp.

Ten minutes after it disappeared I heard leaves rustling about 75 yards down the ridgeline. Moments later I spotted a flicker of movement and knew it was a deer. I then tried to determine whether it wore headgear. The deer turned out to be a 2½-year-

The author once believed that going deeper into forests and big woods almost always meant better hunting than what could be found closer to the road.

Deep-woods whitetails know human voices, slamming car doors, and the rumble of vehicles on roads and trails all mean potential danger.

old buck, and it fed on acorns about 15 minutes before sauntering to another destination. That ended my wildlife sightings for the evening.

WHEN DEEPER WAS BETTER

That bowhunt took place in Wisconsin's North Woods in the mid-1980s, and the stand was one of many I used far from the nearest road. Back then, I thought going deep into the woods almost guaranteed better hunting. Of course, I was younger then, so walking the "extra mile" meant nothing to me. Also, hunting pressure was then virtually non-existent in many

104

forests I bowhunted. Not only that, but I saw enough big-buck activity throughout the season to keep me believing deeper truly was better. But man, have things changed!

Before proceeding with this "deeper-is-better" discussion, let's agree this is a case where "always" and "never" seldom apply. Although I'll explain why deeper isn't necessarily better, let's also agree it's true for some places and times.

OK. Let's move on. The wary nature of mature big-woods bucks has often made me scratch my head, especially during my early hunting days. I sometimes attributed their on-edge behavior to human presence, but I eventually came to believe it's just the natural make-up of trophy bucks. After all, hunting pressure, especially bowhunting pressure, seldom exceeded "light" in my area. Big bucks are just naturally suspicious and skittish.

Still, humans were a factor to some degree. Big-woods whitetails know that human voices, slamming doors, and vehicles buzzing by on nearby roads all mean potential danger. I also learned big-woods whitetails know long distances between themselves and humans almost always create safety and solitude. Though they might wander near roads, fields and back yards during darkness — fresh rubs and scrapes tell the tale — they'll be in their distant sanctuaries by first light.

I remember many mile-or-better early-morning jaunts to try to catch big bucks slipping into their bedding areas at first light. In fact, my plans often succeeded. But in many cases the pre-dawn light wasn't enough to illuminate my sight pins. Talk about frustration! With the exception of the rut and late pre-rut, bucks I hunted pretty much shut down within a half-hour of first light. That meant I usually had at least 30 minutes of hard walking to reach spots that would be productive for 30 minutes. And then I had another 30-minute walk when the morning hunt ended, followed by a repeat performance in the evening.

My first experience with a big buck that didn't play the "deeper-is-better" game occurred during the late 1980s. I was making yet another mile-long morning hike out of the woods when I started finding steaming-fresh big-buck sign. At first there were only scattered rubs and scrapes, but as I neared the road I noticed a lot more sign. I was just about within sight of my vehicle when a huge buck exploded from a clump of dogwood brush.

I stared slack-jawed as the brute crashed over a ridgetop. After waiting for my heart to stop pounding, I looked around. What I found shocked and surprised me.

It was apparent the monster whitetail was living within sight of the township road where I was parked. At first, I was surprised a mature deer would make its home in such a spot, but I eventually pieced together the puzzle, and it made sense. From its bedding spot in the alders, the buck could watch everything on the road, which lay to the east. And with autumn's predominant westerly winds, the buck's nose could monitor everything in the forest behind him. The only reason I'd been able to slip in on him that morning was because a rare easterly wind was blowing.

What else motivated the buck to bed there? Judging by what my scouting revealed, I believe the pressure I had been applying in the deep woods forced the buck closer to the road. I had become my own worst enemy! That trophy buck opened my eyes. I quit assuming mature bucks lived "way back in," and it's a darned good thing I did. As I was about to discover, mature buck behavior in that area was about to undergo dramatic changes.

WHY DEEPER ISN'T ALWAYS BETTER

I could sum up this part of the chapter by saying mature whitetails prefer to hang out where they know they'll usually be left alone. Years ago, that would have meant they stayed deep inside the woods, but that's not the case anymore, at least not where I hunt. It was amazing to watch the transition that occurred when my hunting areas started "shrinking," mostly from logging. I'm not implying that logging didn't help whitetails and other wildlife in that part of the world, however. It most certainly did.

Huge chunks of mature forest, some more than a mile across, were often clearcut in one swoop. Deer numbers, which were dismal before the logging occurred, soon exploded. The area went from about 10 deer per square mile to more than 25 deer per square mile. It was a dream-come-true for big-woods bowhunting, or so I thought. To haul in equipment and haul out their product, the loggers had to build roads, and I don't mean narrow trails. Their roads often allow semi-trailer trucks to get in and out of the forest with few problems. Rather than hauling out

Judging by buck sign the author sometimes finds, it's apparent some giant whitetails live within sight of roads where he parks his truck.

Logging companies and the U.S. Forest Service often build roads wide and strong to allow semi-trailer trucks to haul heavy equipment and wood products from deep within forests and big woods.

logs, these guys set up huge chipping machines deep inside the forest and fed them logs. The chips were then blown into covered semi-trailers and hauled to a distant wood-products factory.

I had mixed feelings toward logging. On one hand, what bowhunter wouldn't want to see deer on every hunt? Not only that, but those new roads into my once-desolate hunting areas made access much easier. Gone were the 30-minute walks to my stands. On the other hand, gone were the days I had those areas to myself. Bowhunting pressure increased dramatically in northwestern Wisconsin's forests. With that overnight increase came deer behaviors I hadn't seen before. Many of the mature bucks relocated for good.

What I found most interesting was that they didn't move to remaining remote areas. Instead, they sought areas that ensured they would avoid repeated run-ins with humans. I got my butt kicked when I first tried to figure out where these bucks went, but I eventually developed a plan for finding them.

The author was amazed to see how quickly mature bucks would go from almost zero tolerance of humans to a certain level of acceptance.

PATTERNING HUNTERS IS VITAL

I had spent a fair amount of time over the years bowhunting farmland whitetails, so I turned to farmland strategies and my insights into how whitetails handle human intrusions. Farmland deer don't head for the hills every time they encounter pressure. I also knew that farmland deer, especially mature bucks, often patterned hunters who pursue them. They know where hunters park their vehicles, where they walk into the woods and, in many instances, where they hang their stands. Big farmland bucks then adjust accordingly.

The big-woods deer I was bowhunting did much the same thing. I was amazed how quickly those once-unpressured bucks altered their lifestyles. I was further amazed how quickly they went from near-zero tolerance of humans to a certain level of acceptance. I'm not saying those once-skittish, reclusive bucks changed personalities. Most of their activities still occurred after dark. They also wouldn't tolerate as much interaction with humans as do farmland deer, but they weren't as quick to take flight as they had been.

Even so, I needed a plan for exploiting their changing behavior, which meant I had to assess how much pressure they encountered from other hunters. I needed to pattern my competition as thoroughly as I had patterned big-woods deer. That hadn't been difficult in my early days because 90 percent of those guys never walked more than a quarter-mile off the nearest road. As logging operations opened the once-roadless forest, however, I couldn't make such assumptions. Hunters could now appear almost anywhere.

Even so, in comparison to mature whitetails, people are a breeze to figure out. They always leave evidence of their passing or presence. Whether it's ATV tracks, candy wrappers, soda cans, cigarette butts, boot prints, snipped walking trails, empty shell casings, or permanent (and illegal) tree stands, my fellow hunters revealed their activities. Their parked vehicles provided another obvious clue about which areas were pressured. During prime hunting hours I drove the roads weaving through my hunting areas. Yes, that sacrificed precious hunting time, but I could then pinpoint which areas were hunted and which were vacant.

Those "scouting" trips also revealed that, almost to a man,

110

Most bowhunters quickly teach whitetails their intentions and travel preferences. After all, people are far more predictable than whitetails, which means a mature buck can usually pattern us long before we pattern him.

111

The author has seen big-woods whitetails abandon an area after discovering highly favored natural foods coming into season in another area.

these guys believed the deeper they went, the better the hunting they would find. With this sudden infusion of way-back hunting pressure, as well as the "loud" behavior some of them displayed, big-buck activity increased nearer the roads. Instead of just visiting the quarter-mile or so of cover near roads, as they once had done, some big bucks now took up residency there.

Fortunately, I caught onto this change quickly, and was amazed how close to the roads some bucks would operate. I moved some of my stands so close to roads that I could see vehicles drive by. I might add that these stands were productive, too! I remember the skepticism of a hunting partner who asked where I was hunting and then refused to believe mature big-woods bucks would hang out near roads. My joking reply went something like this: "I like to be close enough to the road to see vehicles drive by, but not so close that I can read their license plates." I wasn't exaggerating much!

I can't stress enough the value of patterning other hunters. I have no doubt that increased hunting pressure deep in the woods caused the bucks I was chasing to suddenly relocate. That's the downside of increasing and improving a forest's roads and trails. They ease everyone's access, not just yours! And be assured, hunting pressure will escalate when once-remote areas — which before couldn't realistically be hunted — suddenly become a short walk from an ATV or 4x4 truck.

IS FOOD THE DECIDING FACTOR?

Although I believe hunting pressure is the No. 1 reason mature bucks often re-establish core areas nearer to roads, bucks will also pull up stakes when highly favored foods come into season in another area. Those shifts only happen, however, when nutritious foods are suddenly available in abundance. Small supplies are quickly consumed, and do not hold deer for long.

When deer find a huge supply of acorns, especially when it's an isolated crop, or they follow the noise of chain saws to a huge cut and fresh browse, you must move with them. If you don't, you'll be in for some long, boring sits. Provided they find bedding cover and secure travel corridors, big-woods deer will temporarily establish small core areas. And in many big-woods regions these days, there's as good chance the core area will be near a road.

I'm reminded of an acorn-laden oak ridge years ago that became the herd's feeding focus. What made that ridge most interesting was that a stand of mature poplars separated its oaks from a dirt road, screening them from passersby. I discovered the oaks while taking an early-morning drive through the area in early September. When I saw lots of fresh tracks crisscrossing the road, I got out and investigated. A well-traveled runway led me through the poplars and to the oaks.

Acorns were just starting to drop and, man, were the deer keyed in! Piles of droppings lay everywhere. I also found fresh rubs and a couple of small scrapes. Best of all, there was no sign of anyone else. The oak ridge was long but not wide, and it held many mature trees, all of which were loaded with acorns. The ridge was bordered on the far end by a wet, thick tamarack swamp. Obviously, the whitetails had everything they needed in one relatively small area: plenty of food, water and bedding cover.

I hunted that ridge off and on the entire archery season, and if memory serves me, I saw deer on every hunt. As I suspected they might, the big bucks showed up once the rut kicked into gear. But try as I might, I couldn't get one of the antlered beauties to walk within bow range. On several occasions I had big bucks near while listening to vehicles rumble by on the nearby road. Talk about an ironic twist on the term "big-woods hunting!"

GOOD OL' DAYS RETURN

Does that mean I seek only easy-to-hunt places that everyone else overlooks? Of course not, but if I find them I don't pass them up. Even so, I admit my hunting preference remains those remote sites where I seldom see or hear signs of other hunters. Fortunately for me, I can still find such sites near home. During the early 2000s, for instance, I began hunting a big-woods region in my home state that hadn't experienced much logging activity. Most of the logging work I've seen consists of scattered 20- to 40-acre select cuts. Also, bowhunting pressure is minimal, and mature bucks have little tolerance for humans. At the first hint of pressure they plunge deeper into the thousands of acres of roadless cover.

As you might imagine, it's paradise to me, and the "deeper-is-

When the author finds several fresh rubs and a couple of scrapes, his next move is to scout further for any sign of other bowhunters working the hotspot.

better" rule still applies. Granted, that can make for tough hunting, but my son, Jake, and I wouldn't have it any other way. To our way of thinking, having the woods to ourselves makes for a quality hunt. In that respect, I would have to say deeper is definitely always better!

115

CHAPTER NINE

TRAILS? WHAT TRAILS?

Whitetails living in forests and big woods tend to be more nomadic than their counterparts in smaller habitats, and this behavior is usually linked to food availability. Most big-woods habitats can't offer the variety and abundance of nutritious foods common to farm country. Big-woods deer learn at a young age they must sometimes travel far to chow down on foods they like best. In most cases, fawns gain this experience by following and learning from their mamas as they move about the forest searching for their next meal.

Before going further let's address any misconceptions about this chapter's title. It's not that deer trails don't exist in forests and deep-woods habitats. In fact, I've found a few big-woods deer trails that were as obvious as any in farm country. At the same time, it's also true forests hold far more "hidden" trails than what's common in farmlands. One obvious reason is that the big woods hold substantially more cover. As a result, deer benefit from some degree of cover no matter where they walk.

That story is different in farmlands because these deer often restrict their travels to specific areas to take advantage of more limited cover. As a result, pronounced trails soon appear when deer after deer use the routes. In addition, farmland trails usually are more obvious because agricultural range almost always holds more deer than do forests and big woods. Obviously, you can expect more rubs, scrapes, tracks and defined trails/runways where deer densities are high.

For those who haven't yet taken the big-woods challenge, I can assure you of one thing: There's a world of difference between

Forest whitetails learn at an early age that they must sometimes travel far to chow down on foods they like the most.

the amount of sign you'll find in areas holding 25 or more deer per square mile and areas holding 15 or fewer deer per square mile. That's the main reason it takes so much more time and effort to become consistently successful as a big-woods bowhunter.

FIGURING OUT WHERE THE BIG BUCKS WALK

One aspect of big-woods buck behavior that caused me more grief than any other is the way mature bucks move about their range. Oh sure, they follow some predictable patterns, but there are just as many, if not more situations, where they're less obvious and almost unpredictable. That can cause even the most experienced big-woods bowhunters to yank out their hair.

This reminds me of a huge 10-pointer I hunted years ago. I chased that deer for two full archery seasons and only once had him anywhere near bow range. The main problem was that he was as "rub-happy" as any buck I've ever pursued, and he loved to rub especially large trees. He would actually go out of his way to rub 6- to 8-inch thick spruce trees.

I put in countless hours during the post-season and spring the first year trying to unravel several of his more common travel routes. I even became fairly confident I had figured out which parts of his range he used at specific times during the archery season, but I eventually discovered I had a lot to learn about this big whitetail.

Although I hunted him exceptionally hard the first season, I only got fleeting glimpses of him, and each encounter followed a similar scenario. First, I'd hear the unmistakable sounds of a walking deer. Next, everything would go silent for a few minutes. Then I'd hear the sound of huge antlers raking brush and grinding on tree trunks. Usually I'd hear a few subtle grunts and then the sounds of the buck walking away.

In every instance that first year the buck made a sudden "detour" from the rub line it had been following — which just happened to be the one where I waited in ambush. Rather than use runways, the buck seemed to walk randomly through the woods. It appeared he wasn't following a runway, nor was he trailing other deer. It was almost as if he suddenly decided to just wander aimlessly through the forest.

118

Bowhunters will find a huge difference in the amount of deer sign in areas with 25 deer per square mile compared to areas with 10 or fewer deer per square mile.

Can you ever find too many rubs? The author recalls a trophy buck that kept things interesting because it was more "rub-happy" than any buck he ever pursued.

During the second season, he showed himself again, but this time I got a real up-close-and-personal look. That encounter on a bitterly cold morning in early November darned near earned him a ride in the back of my pickup. As usual, I was set up along one of his more active rub lines. About 30 minutes after daylight I heard a large branch break in thick brush behind my stand. A few seconds later a loud, deep grunt echoed through the woods. Then I heard the sounds of a deer walking through frozen leaves.

The sounds told me that he was heading my way. It was obvious, however, that rather than following his rub line, he was walking through a tangled jungle of dogwood brush to my left. It appeared he was again just meandering through the woods. I listened intently as he drew closer, and eventually spotted a flash of gray through the brush. The buck took a few more steps and I made out the left side of a huge set of antlers. Before I knew it, the huge trophy was broadside at 15 yards! Try as I might, I could not find an opening large enough to slip an arrow through.

The buck stood motionless nearly a minute. The wind seemed perfect and I was frozen in place, yet somehow the buck figured out something wasn't quite right. (Now, I don't know what other bowhunters might think, but I'm convinced that prey animals, especially whitetails, possess a sixth sense that sometimes warns them of imminent threats.) The buck became visibly more alert and suspicious as the seconds ticked away. Eventually he turned and disappeared back into the dogwoods. I didn't know it at the time, but that was the end of my chase for that buck. He was killed by a gun hunter a couple of weeks later.

Had the buck approached along the rub line where my stand was located, I would have had a clear 10-yard shot. But just as I'd seen him do before, he cut a few corners and approached through the dogwoods. He was about to pick up his rub line again when he figured out danger was near.

Although it appeared the buck wasn't following a runway when he took off on his jaunt straight at me, closer investigation proved he was indeed on a runway. However, runways like that are usually so subtle that I must stand on them before seeing them. That was the case this time, too.

As my big-woods experience increased, I noticed some of these corridors held small amounts of buck sign, but just as often I found no evidence a buck occasionally passes through. In fact, I still have trouble finding these secret passageways — at least when trying to locate them purely by scouting. The main problem is that there's usually no obvious features readily identifying these corridors. It's simply not possible to study an area from a distance and pick out likely spots. That doesn't mean, however, that one can only speculate about their location or existence.

OBSERVATIONS ARE CRITICAL TO SUCCESS

As I mentioned in an earlier chapter, I always prefer actual observations for pinpointing buck travel routes when hunting in or near clearings. I should have added that I put great stock in actual observations no matter where I'm hunting in a forest or big woods! Nothing tells me more conclusively where big bucks like to walk. That's why I urge bowhunters to totally tune into their surroundings every moment they're in their tree stands. Given how little sign big bucks sometimes leave, observations are the only way you'll get an exact line on how they traverse their ranges.

Without such sightings, it's sometimes difficult to figure out why big-woods bucks often make sudden deviations from travel routes and seemingly take off cross-country. In some cases, they're just veering off to take a shortcut to a specific destination. They know the shortest distance between two points is a straight line, and sometimes they'll take it even if it requires a little more effort. That might explain why rub/scrape lines are seldom straight for long. Most rub/scrape lines I've unraveled over the decades make many twists and turns.

But make no mistake: As with farmland deer, big-woods whitetails start their evening jaunts at a definite Point A, their bedding areas; and for most of autumn head off toward a definite Point B, usually a distant food source. In most situations they stick close to their preferred travel routes for these walks. We shouldn't assume, however, that deer never change their minds or get in a hurry to reach their destination. That's when they take a straighter line of travel, which usually involves a hidden runway.

I've noticed a critical fact about this aspect of buck travel: In

The author recalls a buck that escaped because it stopped where it was well-screened by trees and brush. Try though he did, the author could not find an opening large enough to slip an arrow through.

123

almost every case the buck starts his evening walk by following one of his rub/scrape lines some distance before veering off cross-country. After all, bucks establish their rub/scrape lines along routes where they feel safe and secure. Even though they might "detour" from these routes eventually, they'll stick to them at first, probably trying to get a read on what's happening in their surroundings. Once they're convinced everything's cool, they'll consider lowering their guard a bit and cutting cross-country.

Big bucks won't walk just anywhere, of course, and they use their hidden travel corridors often enough to make it worth your time and effort to find them. This is where your observations must not be ignored. I've talked with dozens of big-woods bowhunters who have seen mature bucks walking through the forest, seemingly at random. In most cases, these bowhunters told me they were set up along an obvious big-buck rub/scrape line when they saw the brute walking in the distance. They passed off the event as bad luck. They didn't even consider relocating their stands. They figured it was just a matter of time before the buck walked by again, the next time within bow range, of course. That might happen, but it might not.

Several factors helped me become a consistently successful big-woods deer hunter, but I think the No. 1 reason is my curiosity. I never stop trying to figure out why big bucks do certain things. It isn't enough to know they sometimes disregard established travel routes and walk through other parts of the woods. I want to know why they do it, and whether it's a behavior I can exploit. I watched several big-woods bucks pull this stunt before I investigated the situation. One thing in my favor was that I paid attention to exactly where the bucks walked. I used logs, downed trees and clumps of brush as landmarks, and then retraced the bucks' routes. Those observations made it much easier to find their hidden trails.

What did I find when I investigated? In some instances the hidden trails ran only a short distance, letting the buck cut the corner of a particular stretch of his normal route. In other cases, the hidden trails ran much farther, letting bucks bypass a substantial part of their normal route and decreasing the time needed to reach their destination. Therefore, their "detours"

The author often reminds bowhunters not to expect obvious deer sign in some forests and deep woods. Bucks in those habitats don't always make or leave obvious evidence of their favorite travel routes.

Mature bucks do not let down their guard and veer cross-country from a time-tested route unless they're convinced everything is cool.

often aren't random, and they're more aptly called shortcuts. That's why it pays to note exactly where bucks walk, and never assume it's a random occurrence. If you never investigate such observations, don't be surprised when bucks continually pass just out of range.

HIDDEN TRAILS AND THE RUT

Once I got serious about unraveling such mysteries, it took only a few years to become proficient at patterning big-woods bucks during the early season and pre-rut. What about the rut? That's a different story. It's very difficult to stay consistent on big-

126

Regardless of how much time and energy it takes to pinpoint "hidden" buck trails, bowhunters will discover it's worth the time and effort.

woods bowhunts during the rut. I haven't had such struggles in farm country during the rut. As the rut approaches in agricultural areas, all one needs to do is pinpoint whitetail family groups. Then it's usually just a matter of time before the biggest bucks show up looking to court estrous does.

In addition, I've never had much difficulty figuring out how farmland bucks move about their ranges during the rut. Farmland bucks use obvious terrain features such as points of timber, brush lines, bottlenecks and ridgelines when cruising. Locating these "cruising corridors" in forests and the deep woods isn't as easy, but they do exist. Once again, you must pay attention every moment you're in the woods. And instead of staying put and hoping a cruising buck walks by within range during his next circuit, locate the hidden trail he used when you spotted him.

Although it might appear otherwise, rutting bucks almost always travel along certain lines when cruising for hot does. More importantly, they'll pretty much follow those lines every time they travel through specific areas. Of course, the problem with waiting along just one of a big buck's travel lines during the rut is that it could be awhile before he reuses that route. Then again, all bowhunters face that dilemma regardless of the habitat they're hunting. It's not unusual for a mature buck to vacate an area for days when the rut is in full swing. Waiting for a targeted buck to repeat a swing through a favored rut haunt can test one's patience. That's especially true in forests and deep woods, where deer sightings during such waits are usually few and far between.

How, then, do I do it? I have confidence I'll be in the right spot when a targeted buck eventually appears, and I've had it happen often enough to know it's worth every bit of my patience. Sure, I've had my share of unproductive hunts while playing the waiting game, but this strategy is as productive as any other big-woods tactic I've used during the rut.

SUMMARY

Just because "hidden" trails are sometimes difficult to locate doesn't mean they aren't worth hunting. Big bucks use them often enough to warrant some of your tree-stand hours. That means it's worth the extra time and effort required to find them.

Although it might appear otherwise at times, rutting bucks almost always follow specific lines through a forest when cruising for hot does.

129

CHAPTER TEN

ARE DEEP-WOODS BUCKS EASY?

A common misconception among bowhunters who have never chased big-woods whitetails is that mature bucks in forests and deep woods are easier to kill. I've heard several theories about that belief, but the most common falsehood is that big-woods bucks are easier prey because they have little experience with humans compared to farmland deer. That supposedly makes them less wary than their farmland counterparts. And, as a result, big-wood bucks are supposedly more easily duped by rattling antlers, grunt calls, and well-placed lures and scents.

If all that's true, I've been doing many things wrong since at least the late 1970s! For starters, my rattling sequences must not sound realistic and my grunt calls must be out of tune. And could the scents and lures I've been using smell too sour for big-woods deer? Somehow I doubt it. In reality, big-woods bucks are anything but pushovers. You don't have to take my word for it. If you pose the question to any bowhunter who has spent more than a few years chasing big-woods whitetails, you'll get an earful about the difficulties of consistently getting within bow range of these creatures.

Before continuing, let me be clear: I do not consider mature farmland bucks to be pushovers, either. Nor am I implying that those who chase farm-country whitetails are somehow second-rate bowhunters. I spend a lot of time each autumn bowhunting agricultural regions, and those whitetails are very challenging!

WHAT MAKES BIG-WOODS BUCKS SO DIFFICULT?

Granted, whitetails in true forests have little or no contact with humans most of the year. In some regions, in fact, it's pos-

Some beginning or uninformed bowhunters believe big-woods bucks are more easily duped by rattling and calling than are farmland bucks.

sible for whitetails to go more than a year without encountering humans. However, that doesn't mean they'll lower their guard even slightly when sniffing or seeing a hunter. Wilderness whitetails know the potential perils of humans.

Some experiences I had during a bowhunt in Alberta, Canada, during the 1990s provide some proof. That hunt took place north of Iron River, Alberta, a region that's a true big-woods setting if ever I saw one. In fact, it's more accurate to call it a wilderness setting. The timber I bowhunted went many miles around without an intruding road. It also held a variety of predators, including lynx, coyotes, bobcats, black bears and timber wolves. In fact, the only predator in short supply was humans, especially during archery season.

From the outset I knew I had never chased whitetails in timber as huge as those Alberta forests. And even though I should have known better, I immediately assumed killing one of the forest's big bucks would be a piece of cake. After all, what experience could they have had with humans? My first hint that things wouldn't be that easy was when a bachelor group of immature bucks passed my stand the first morning. I spotted this cavalcade of young antlers when they emerged from thick poplar brush 75 yards away. The five whitetails walked within 15 yards of the thick pine that held my stand.

That's when I first realized the way this hunt might go. The light wind on that late October morning was blowing from the bucks to me. My portable stand was a good 15 feet off the ground, and I was nestled among thick cover to my sides and behind. Even so, as is always the case when I have deer around me, I didn't take anything for granted, and remained absolutely still. Unbelievably, one of the bucks picked me off in the pine. His reaction was immediate and surprising. Rather than doing the characteristic head-bob and/or stare-down, the 8-pointer snorted loudly, whirled and, with his four buddies in tow, crashed away into a spruce thicket.

Wow! Talk about getting your bubble burst! There I was bowhunting whitetails in a pristine setting — one where they had never seen a tree stand before — and I got picked off in the first 30 minutes. You'd better believe that encounter changed my expectations of what it would take to shoot a mature buck in those woods! In fact, I never did arrow a big buck on that hunt. I didn't

The author should have known better, but he once assumed big bucks in a wilderness area he was hunting would be pushovers. He soon discovered these supposedly unpressured bucks were as wary as any white-tailed bucks he had hunted.

133

It's difficult to predict when bucks will respond to calling and rattling. The author recalls several occasions when he saw bucks acting very "rutty," yet they seldom responded to calling and rattling strategies.

even come close. But I did see a couple of exceptional animals. Never in my life have I worked as hard for a big deer as I did on that eight-day hunt. I arose each day at 3 a.m., was out the door by 3:45, and never returned until nearly 8 o'clock each night.

Another interesting, and frustrating, fact was that those whitetails mostly didn't respond to rattling and grunting. What puzzled me the most was that the bucks displayed definite pre-rut behavioral traits. Every day of the hunt the outfitter and I found fresh scrapes and rubs, more than just few of which were on 4- to 6-inch trees. We also saw fair numbers of antlerless deer and immature bucks each day. On several occasions we even saw immature bucks scraping, rubbing, trailing and chasing does. In general, they were acting very "rutty." Yet try as I might, I couldn't get a mature buck to respond to my calling.

Knowing the caliber of the bucks in that region only made the situation more frustrating. Not only that, but the region's harsh winters and abundant predators kept the herd's buck-to-doe ratio as tight as any I've seen in the wild. One would think the balanced sex ratio would have created great rattling/calling scenarios, but I never saw it.

I'm not implying that rattling and calling can't be productive for big-woods bowhunters. It most certainly can be. What I'm saying is that in areas with low deer densities, one shouldn't expect high response rates. In other words, it's tough to call in a big buck when no big bucks hear your calling efforts. But when a big buck is within hearing range, and provided it's the right time of year, there's a good chance you'll generate a response. The nearly even buck-to-doe ratios so often found in the big woods create more breeding competition among mature bucks. As always, the greater the competition, the greater the chance for positive responses to calling.

As always, thorough scouting of your hunting areas plays a crucial role in calling and rattling. Take it from someone who learned the hard way, setting up just anywhere and hoping a mature buck or two hears you is just a shot in the dark. To increase response rates, you must scout to learn where big bucks prefer to bed, travel and feed, and then establish your setups accordingly. And trust me: In the big woods, there's far more country that's unproductive than vice-versa.

Bowhunters must keep several guidelines uppermost in their minds when using scents and lures. Of primary importance is keeping human scent off everything they touch when applying scents.

CHAPTER TEN: ARE DEEP-WOODS BUCKS EASY?

VALUABLE TIDBITS OF INFORMATION

Earlier in this chapter I mentioned that I use scents and lures for big-woods bowhunts. I use them because I've done well with them. However, judging by feedback I've heard over the years, this aspect of bowhunting is widely misunderstood, especially when bowhunting big-woods whitetails.

I believe two aspects of scent and lure usage cost bowhunters more big bucks than all others combined. First, some hunters believe mature bucks can't wait to investigate the scent's source when they catch a whiff of these magic potions. They think it's pretty much a done deal at that point. I don't believe that for a minute. I have no idea what "additional ingredients" go into commercially manufactured deer scents and lures. I do know, however, that some scents work, some scents don't, and no scent works every time. That's because situations and circumstances in the woods vary greatly by buck, by region, by time of season, by time of day, and by individual hunter.

Why do some hunters believe big-woods bucks are especially susceptible to scents and lures? Personally, I've hunted both environments extensively, and I'll never believe big-woods bucks are more prone than their farmland cousins to falling for commercially manufactured deer scents/lures. Even so, I know not everyone agrees. As one guy told me: "Big-woods deer haven't been exposed to scents and lures the way farmland deer have, so the stuff should work a lot better on them. Right?"

I nodded in polite agreement, but asked: "So, you're telling me it really doesn't matter what's in a scent or lure; or how, where or when it's used? It's just a matter of having a big-woods buck get downwind of the stuff, and it's pretty much a done deal. Is that right?"

He said that was exactly what he meant, and continued: "You gotta admit, Greg, there's a lotta competition for breeding rights in the big woods. The way I see it, anything that smells even a little like an estrous doe has to be effective. Every mature buck on the prowl can't help but check it out."

The guy's reasoning appears sensible on the surface, but I think it's fraught with unproven assumptions. I'm here to tell you that applying commercially produced estrous scent into a mature buck's domain does not guarantee quick success. And that's a fact that applies no matter where you hunt big deer.

The other large factor concerns our own odors. In fact, I think careless attitudes about human scent are the No. 1 reason so many hunters have little faith in scents and lures. When they see a deer react with alarm to a scent or lure they've applied, they don't realize the deer is responding to human scent left behind, not the actual deer scent or lure. I learned that lesson the hard way. In fact, I remember many bad experiences with scents and lures in my early big-woods bowhunts.

Most of those bad experiences resulted from my own careless behavior, and one experience springs to mind. It happened in late October, the peak pre-rut time in Wisconsin's North Woods. My intention on that frosty morning was to lay a scent line along my walking trail, ending it at a canister 15 yards from my stand. The canister contained the same scent and was hanging about waist-high.

About a half-hour after daylight I heard a deer walking through frozen leaves that lay ankle deep on the forest floor. I barely had time to grab my bow from its hanger when the deer walked into view. One glance told me it was a buck, and a definite shooter. That glance also told me the buck was following the scent line I'd laid down that morning. I could tell from the buck's demeanor he would follow the scent line to the canister, at which point I would shoot. I turned and got into position while sneaking glances as the big buck drew closer.

That buck was as enamored with that scent as any deer I've ever duped with the stuff. He was grunting and drooling, and he had the glassy-eyed look of an animal that seems oblivious to its surroundings. In other words, the situation appeared to be a done deal. As the buck extended his neck to sniff the canister, I began drawing. I had barely started putting tension on the string when everything went south. The 10-pointer gave a short, loud snort and exploded out of there as if he'd been zapped with a cattle prod. I sat down on my tree stand and tried to figure out what the heck had happened. At first I thought the scent I'd used somehow spooked the buck. Just as quickly, I knew that wasn't the case. After all, the buck had followed that very scent to the canister.

As I looked down at the canister, it dawned on me what had happened. Before hanging it on the bush, I had broken off a few branches that got in the way. Although I knew better, I hadn't been wearing gloves. The buck, therefore, had gotten a nose full of "Perfume de

138

Merely introducing white-tailed doe estrous scent or other "sure-fire" scents into your big-woods area does not guarantee quick success. These bucks aren't any more susceptible to scents than are bucks in farmland areas with large herds.

Greg Miller," and his reaction had been instant fear and flight.

Based on such experiences, I'd wager many hunters err when assuming scents and lures caused deer to suddenly bolt. In almost every instance, I'd bet the deer was fleeing from something else, and it's probably human odor.

Remember, too, that mature farmland bucks are just as leery of our odors. They're well-schooled in where to expect such smells, and don't hesitate to flee when they encounter them in the wrong place. Given that, consider what you're up against with big-woods deer. They grow up believing human odor ain't supposed to be anywhere! The slightest whiff sends them packing.

TREAD LIGHTLY!

OK, so it's a given big-woods deer are sensitive to human odor. Therefore, it only stands to reason that bowhunters must go the extra mile to control their smells. Although most bowhunters have improved in this care in recent years, there's room for improvement. That shortcoming is most obvious in how bowhunters walk through the woods and forests. Many of the same people who spend hours, days or even weeks trying to figure out where to place their stands spend little time figuring out the best route to reach those sites. In too many cases they simply take the shortest, most direct route.

More times than not, such decisions cost you big time. I can't stress enough the importance of a covert approach when bowhunting mature big-woods bucks. These bucks are tough to hunt even when they have no idea they're being hunted. Once they realize they're being pursued, they're virtually impossible to kill.

My early attempts at ambushing forest bucks were exercises in futility. Looking back, it's easy to pinpoint some of my glaring mistakes. In the worst instances, I tipped my hand to bucks before I even started hunting them. I routinely walked through deer-activity areas while walking to and from my stands. By the time the best part of bow season arrived, the bucks I was hunting knew far more about me than I did about them. They knew where I walked, where I stood and, in some instances, when I was on stand.

My success rate started rising the first year I took a more secretive approach. I became fanatical about keeping my body and clothing as odor-free as possible. Second, I became extremely careful about where I walked. It might sound far-fetched to some, but I often walked nearly a mile out of my way to keep from bumping deer while walking in and out. Such hikes might be difficult to justify at first, but they'll greatly improve your big-woods bowhunts. Never forget that big-woods bucks are anything but easy!

The author recalls sitting down on his tree stand after a heartbreaking close encounter, and trying to figure out what went wrong. He concluded the buck had gotten a nose full of "Perfume de Greg Miller."

CHAPTER ELEVEN

DEEP-WOODS RUB LINES

I've seen a ton of deer hunting strategies come and go during my 40-plus years of chasing whitetails. Some strategies were more than a bit off base. A select few, however, were on the mark. The best strategies aren't mysterious. In most cases, they're relatively easy to learn and apply, and they're fairly productive.

The problem with most "new" strategies is that they were conceived, tried and tested in farm country. In case you've missed one of the more important themes of this book, let me reaffirm there's a huge difference between forests and farmlands. Then again, it's more accurate to say that whitetails in these two environments demonstrate huge behavioral differences. The most significant difference is their varying tolerances for humans. In a sense, farm-country whitetails live among and somewhat depend on humans for food via agricultural crops and plantings. On the flip side, big-woods deer will eat foods that man provides through logging, artificial feeding, and scattered farms, but they tend to be far more self-reliant, surviving with or without such aid.

Because farm-country whitetails are accustomed to being around humans and agricultural food sources, they're easier to scout than big-woods deer. For example, my hunting partners and I have an annual ritual in my home state. Around mid-August, we often get together in southwestern Wisconsin and drive rural roads during the last hour or so of daylight, video-taping some of the big bucks that pack into alfalfa and soybean fields. It's an incredible experience, trust me. We also bowhunt some of the farms where we've seen those big bucks. Talk about a great way to keep a running tab on the quality and quantity of big bucks! There's nothing like sightings of monster deer to get your adrenaline flowing!

Those mid-August inventories have led to some interesting

Farm-country whitetails spend most of their lives in close proximity to humans, often eating agricultural crops and other foods we plant. Forest deer, meanwhile, might go for weeks, months and even years between encounters with humans. As a result, bowhunters should expect vast behavioral differences between big-woods deer and farmland deer.

Many big-woods bucks the author has tagged were "strangers" to him until seconds before he released his arrow. Even though he had never seen the bucks before, the author knew they existed because they left rubs and rub lines around the forest.

discoveries over the years, because these mature bucks often undergo many changes between the time we videotape them and when archery season opens a month later. The most notable discovery is that they often seem to fall off the face of the earth until late October and early November. At one time that caused me to grow frustrated and irritated, but no longer. I eventually learned to remind myself of how things usually go in the big woods, and that reality check changes my attitude instantly. Anytime you get a preseason look at a big buck you'll later hunt, you're miles ahead of normal, but rarely does that happen when hunting forests and deep woods.

Many big-woods bucks I've killed were strangers to me until seconds before I dropped the string on them. That doesn't mean I was unaware they existed. Although I never actually saw them until that moment, I knew a heck of a lot about most of them.

RUB LINES ARE THE KEY

Again, that fact points to my lifelong efforts to hone my sign-interpretation skills to a fine edge. And make no mistake: Those skills aren't developed overnight. They require years of leg-weary scouting trips and patient analysis of every shred of deer sign you find. But you'd better believe attaining such skills is worth the time and effort.

I also know my skills aren't unique. Almost anyone can learn to read and decipher big-buck sign. At no time is that more true than when analyzing antler rubs. Rubs and rub lines are the most important clues we can find for deciphering big-woods bucks. How important? Put it this way: If someone said I could not use rubs and rub lines for getting a line on big-woods bucks, I might just have to quit bowhunting forests and deep woods!

Because sightings of big bucks are rare in the big woods, it's vital to have other ways to assess hunting areas. This is where a basic understanding of rubs and rub lines is essential. Rubs provide insight into the quality and, perhaps, quantity of bucks in a given area. Obviously, all bucks make rubs, but some hunters are a bit foggy when correlating rubs with buck size. I'm often asked if big rubs truly mean big bucks. You bet they do! I can almost guarantee that if a big buck is living within an area he'll make some big rubs there. It's just the nature of the beast.

But using antler rubs as scouting aids goes beyond size correlations. Rubs can help you figure out where big-woods bucks bed, travel and feed. Such information goes a long way toward positioning you to harvest monster bucks. Bucks make new rubs and revisit old rubs pretty much every day they carry hard antlers, and most rubs are found near the outside of their bedding areas and along travel routes throughout their home ranges. Rubs found along their travel routes, when linked together, are the makings of rub lines.

Most of my upcoming discussion focuses on rub lines that link bedding and feeding areas. And because these rub lines can be productive to hunt, I'll also brief you on less-conspicuous rub lines big-woods bucks establish during the rut. Before going further, let's not forget another vital point: As with other aspects of big-woods bowhunting, the best time to scout and unravel rub lines is during the post-season and/or spring.

How can a review of rubs from the previous season reveal the best way to bowhunt future seasons? Quite simply, white-tailed bucks are creatures of habit. Barring major landscape changes to their range, they'll pretty much hang out in the same places, doing the same things, at the same times, year after year. For example, during the mid-1980s I found a rub line in a favorite area in northwestern Wisconsin, and then shot a nice buck off that rub line the first year. My brother Mike arrowed another buck off that rub line the next year, and my brother Jeff took his turn the following year. In fact, my brothers and I killed six bucks off that rub line over an eight-year stretch.

Not only that, but those numbers reflect only the bucks we killed. Conservatively speaking, we saw another couple-dozen bucks during those years, including several monsters. We shot at some and missed, while others walked by out of range and others just gave us the slip.

SCOUTING & DECIPHERING RUB LINES

As they do with scrapes, all bucks living within a given area work many of the same rubs. This fact is important. Although big-woods bucks might roam thousands of acres, the bulk of their activities occur in small areas for most of the year.

As a result, you should expect to see mostly unproductive land

146

If someone were to tell the author he could not use rubs and rub lines to plan his bowhunts, he might be forced to turn his back on forests and deep woods. Without such clues, bowhunting the big woods would be too random and frustrating.

147

when scouting. The big-woods challenge is pinpointing the specific areas deer are using in autumn. To that end, rubs and rub lines provide more reliable clues than any other deer sign, partly because no other deer sign is so visible. That's especially true during the post-season and springtime. Foliage and underbrush are never more bare, dramatically increasing visibility in the woods. This makes it possible to scout large chunks of cover in a short time.

Even so, you won't achieve consistent success along big-woods rub lines if all you do is hunt small parts of them. As my bowhunting partners and I discovered, to be in the game all season we must know where all rub lines – whether they're morning or evening travel routes — begin and end. That's another reason to do your rub-line scouting in the off-season. The last thing you want to do is stumble around your favorite areas during bow season, alerting mature bucks that you're looking for them.

To find rub lines during the off-season I first look at topo maps and aerial photos. I'm looking for topographical features that might funnel deer activity or offer prime bedding areas in the form of benches, swamp islands and other attractive features. I also check around for recent logging activity and other likely feeding areas. After pinpointing several likely looking spots, my legwork begins. My only agenda item for these initial scouting missions is to find as many rubs as I can while covering as much ground as possible.

As I increase my understanding of the lay of the land, my goal is to figure out how bucks use their surroundings. I'll use my maps and photos to mark rubs I find, and to note the locations of terrain features that catch my eye without being visible on my maps or photos. It's amazing how much I can learn about rub-line patterns by studying notes I make on my maps and photos. By sketching in all relevant details, I'm better able to piece together the beginnings, ends and middles of most rub lines. The importance of such information will soon become apparent.

Once I've studied the rub patterns on my maps and photos, I return to the area. Now it's time to try to figure out and pinpoint where each rub line starts, ends and weaves through the forest. I also try to figure out if each rub line is used in the mornings or evenings. As fast as I might have moved on the first scouting mis-

Without a doubt, big rubs indicate the presence of big bucks. But using rubs and rub lines to improve your bowhunting strategies goes far beyond correlating rub size to buck size.

sion, I now slow down just as dramatically for my return visit. Because I now grasp the lay of the land, I focus exclusively on finding more rubs, especially those that help put together all the puzzle pieces.

Following rub lines from beginning to end in a forest can be extremely difficult, because rub lines often twist and curl their way for long distances. About the time I think I reach the end of a rub line, I often spot another rub ahead. In those cases, the search continues. That's why I keep telling myself I might spend an entire

No other type of buck sign stands out as boldly in the woods as rubs. When scouting, mark the location of impressive rubs on your topo maps or aerial photos. You'll be amazed by the patterns that become obvious as you mark down rub locations.

The author never stops looking for topographical features that could indicate prime bedding areas for big bucks. Islands in swamps, benches on hillsides and isolated patches of cover might indicate big-buck bedrooms.

day or two — or many more — trying to unravel one rub line. That's just the way it is. Of course, I take comfort in knowing that when I eventually figure out a rub line, it could produce chances at mature bucks for years to come. That's also just the way it is!

I advise carrying a roll of fluorescent surveyor's tape when scouting rub lines. Remember, you'll be following rubs that will be on the rub-tree's opposite side as you pass by in search of the next rub. As a result, you'll often lose track of the previous rub if you didn't mark it. Surveyor's tape on a nearby branch gives you the luxury of looking back and re-establishing the proper line.

In most instances I can locate bedding and feeding areas on my first scouting trips. This is crucial information to know when returning for a more thorough study of rub lines. Knowing where whitetails feed and bed also helps you determine if a particular rub line is a morning or evening travel route. Figuring out a rub line's travel direction is easy. As most bowhunters know, rubs on a rub line face away from a buck's direction of travel. As you walk through the woods locating rubs, you're traveling in the same direction the buck walked as he made the rubs. Rub lines whose rubs face away from feeding areas almost always are

151

Rub lines often follow edge cover and topographical features. Several generations of bucks might take the same route. Unless something drastic alters the landscape, some rub lines will produce shots at trophy bucks for many consecutive seasons.

evening travel routes, while rub lines whose rubs face toward a feeding area almost always are used for morning travel.

What kind of rub lines draw my attention? Earlier I mentioned that big rubs indicate big bucks. For that reason, I restrict my rub-line scouting missions to rub lines that feature large rubs. I'm not saying every rub along the line must be on a 4- to 6-inch diameter tree. Shoot, I'm just happy to find an occasional rub-tree that size along any rub line I scout. That tells me there's at least one big buck hanging out.

WHERE AND WHEN TO HUNT RUB LINES

I'm often asked the best time to hunt rub lines. In my opinion, there is no bad time to wait in ambush along an active big-woods rub line. I must add, however, that some sections of a rub line produce far more buck sightings than others. It all hinges on the time of season. During the early bow season, your best chance for big-buck activity is near the very edges of bedding areas, whether it's morning or evening. That advice applies through the dreaded "October Lull."

But things loosen up considerably as we near the pre-rut peri-

152

The late pre-rut is a great time to bowhunt stands along the midsections of rub lines. By that time, it's possible to see big-buck action during morning and evening bowhunts.

od. At this time it's not unusual to catch mature bucks moving along their rub lines some distance away from their bedding areas long before dusk. Also, big bucks now often linger at feeding areas in the morning. Therefore, it's possible to see big bucks during morning or evening hunts near the midsections of rub lines.

The pre-rut is also an effective time to try calling. In fact, rattling can be so deadly that I won't walk into any rub-line bowhunt during the pre-rut without rattling antlers. In the big woods, "tight" buck-to-doe ratios create intense competition among breeding-age bucks. In addition, if there's one place bigwoods bucks feel safe and secure when approaching a buck fight, it's along one of their rub lines.

In fact, many bowhunters fail to call in mature bucks because they set up where no whitetail can be coaxed to approach. But when you set up along active rub lines, you're calling from sites where deer believe they're safe. That's why they rubbed there! As I've stressed, big bucks don't rub just anywhere. Even a quick study of rub patterns helps illustrate that fact. Mature bucks do most of their rubbing in select spots, sites where they feel secure enough to lower their guard to make a ruckus and mangle a tree or two.

RUB LINES AND THE RUT

No, the above sub-heading isn't a typo. Remember, a scant few rub lines in the forest or deep woods will see activity from mature bucks during the rut. Just as a reminder, these rub lines are found along the "hidden" runways bucks use when cruising from one area to another. Setting up along this type of rub line during the rut can be darned productive. Trouble is, these are the most difficult rub lines to find and follow.

My experience indicates it's not unusual for rub lines along hidden runways to run well over a mile. And the fact they're long isn't the only challenge of finding and figuring out these hotspots. The rubs themselves are usually few and far between because rutting bucks cruising hidden trails are more concerned with making tracks than making rubs.

Even so, I believe the rewards justify every drop of perspiration you sweat when scouting these rub lines. Other than waiting in ambush near deer family groups, I can't think of a more productive spot to set up for rutting big-woods bucks.

The main reason many bowhunters fail to call in mature bucks is because they rattle and call from places no self-respecting buck would ever approach. That's why it pays to call from areas where you find rubs and scrapes. Those signs tell you bucks feel comfortable there.

CHAPTER TWELVE

THE DEEP-WOODS RUT

I'll start this chapter by saying the big-woods rut can be one of the most exciting experiences a bowhunter could ever imagine. Unfortunately, the big-woods rut can also be one of the most depressing experiences a bowhunter could ever endure. Which experience you have depends on the moment.

Obviously, the rut is a fickle time to bowhunt big bucks in any setting. That's because mature bucks pretty much abandon patterns they established in early autumn. Not only that, but they often abandon their core areas once breeding begins. That situation is an especially tough nut to crack in forests and deep woods because big-timber bucks are far more "nomadic" than their farmland counterparts. When they decide to take a walk to search for hot does, they really take a walk! And that's only one of many differences between the farmland rut and big-woods rut.

Although I've spent lots of time bowhunting farmland deer, I was blessed to get an early start in big-woods bowhunting. Those early years provided great insights into the differences between these environments. One of those insights is that when you're focused on mature, big-woods bucks, you must believe you're no ordinary deer hunter. You must believe you're a special breed of bowhunter. You know going into every situation that the odds strongly favor your quarry. Not only that, but you wouldn't have it any other way.

We know, for example, that we probably won't see many deer. We also know we'll spend more time and walk more miles than we would elsewhere. And most importantly, we accept that our

156

Big-woods bucks are more nomadic than their farmland counterparts. When they decide to take a walk, they can really take a walk!

157

The author will never forget the action he saw in a big-woods bottleneck the first couple of days he sat there. The red-hot action began just after daylight and lasted until the end of legal shooting hours.

tags won't be filled every year. That's the nature of these hunts.

Why do I harp on those facts? Because I've seen so many bowhunters demoralized by the forest's demands. Even during the rut, big-woods bowhunters endure down times that don't even come close to being "so-so days." It's likely you'll go through several deerless days, even during the rut. That's mentally taxing, even for the most self-confident bowhunter.

I'll always remember a tough big-woods rut I went through years ago. It occurred during the first week of November, traditionally the kick-off for rutting activity in northwestern Wisconsin. I was hunting one of my favorite spots, and had my stand set up in a bottleneck of high ground between two large tamarack swamps. The action the first couple of days bordered on unbelievable. I saw bucks chasing does, does chasing bucks, bucks chasing bucks, and several other bucks simply cruising through. The action started just after daylight and lasted through the end of legal shooting time. I saw several shooter bucks those two days, but couldn't get one to walk through the right spot. That was frustrating, but I remained confident things would eventually fall into place.

I couldn't have been more wrong! My third day in the bottleneck didn't produce one deer. Heck, I didn't even hear one! Believing things could only get better, I headed back to the bottleneck on Day 4. I again drew a big fat zero!

It would be natural to assume the spot "burned out" because of my repeated visits, but I'm confident that didn't happen. My body and clothes were as clean and odor-free as humanly possible. I had also made sure my walks into the spot and back out took me through dead zones in the forest. Not only that, but the wind had favored me all four days.

OK, so what happened? Quite simply, the area I was hunting ceased being the center of the action. There wasn't a hint of rutting activity anywhere near the bottleneck. I'd hunted the big woods long enough to know the bucks I'd seen earlier were likely tearing up the forest miles away. That's the nature of the big-woods rut.

WHAT ABOUT SCRAPE LINES AND RUB LINES?

The biggest negative about hunting the big-woods rut is that mature bucks pretty much quit relating to sign. Rub lines and scrape lines that were hot during the final pre-rut days are suddenly devoid of buck activity. With the exception of an occasional visit by an immature buck, you'll be hard-pressed to see activity.

Why? For the most part, mature bucks establish scrape lines and rub lines along travel routes linking their bedding and feeding areas. Rubbing and scraping along these routes helps them track antlered activity within their core areas. One sniff at a scrape or rub tells a buck whether other bucks visited the spot recently. But once the rut kicks into gear, mature bucks lose interest in food and focus their interests on females. And although it might appear otherwise, mature bucks still won't take any more steps than necessary when searching for receptive mates.

Once again, it's now critical to know the exact location of hidden trails, because mature bucks are notorious for taking straight lines when cruising for females. Rather than walking just anywhere when in the cruise mode, rutting bucks use specific routes that save time and energy. We've already dedicated enough space to finding hidden runways. Instead, let's discuss how to best hunt these places during the rut. This subject really isn't too complicated. At risk of becoming repetitive, the best way to bowhunt hidden runways during the rut is to find a quality setup, plant your butt and be patient. Although you can't predict when a rutting buck might come by, it's a good bet you'll spend lots of uneventful time on stand, no matter where you set up. I steel myself to that possibility by realizing if a big buck cruises through, he'll walk right in front of me.

I have a system for determining which of the many hidden trails offers the best chance for a shot at a big buck. It's not foolproof, but the system has worked often enough that I stick with it. I start with a quick walk-around in my hunting areas to see which hidden runways hold the most fresh rub sign. I then narrow the options further by concentrating on runways with the most large rubs.

One benefit of sitting along hidden runways during the rut is that you might see several bucks during one hunt. When no estrous does are available in a given area, every buck around will

One sniff at a rub or scrape can tell a big buck which other bucks, if any, have visited the spot in recent days.

161

be cruising. Those bucks often use the same travel corridors when jumping from one area to another. If you're in the right place at the right time, the action can be incredible. Again, though, you must be patient. The action often blows hot and cold.

WHY RUTTING BUCKS ARE WANDERERS

Never forget that rutting bucks are on a mission, and that they must check lots of country quickly and efficiently. They're literally starving themselves all the while, making it crucial they conserve energy by not wasting steps. Mature bucks know where doe family groups will be hanging out during the rut, and they take the most direct routes between these groups, cutting cross-country whenever possible. As they approach each doe hotspot, they circle downwind and quickly scent-check every antlerless deer they can find. If they detect one in estrus or nearing estrus, they single her out and "cut" her from the group. The chase is on!

But if they don't detect estrous scent, rutting bucks don't wait for a change in status. They soon head out to another area that holds antlerless deer. This is where, from a bowhunting standpoint, a major problem can occur. You see, unlike farm country where doe numbers are almost always higher and more concentrated, the next family group could be far away. If estrous does are again absent, the buck keeps traveling.

I can cite many cases where big-woods bucks I hunted in one area got killed by someone else miles away. How many miles? Well, a friend of mine provides an extreme example. He was bowhunting for a particular buck during the pre-rut, only to verify it was killed by a car more than 13 miles away during the rut. This buck carried a large 10-point rack and a third main beam, so identifying it was as certain as a finger print!

The challenge of exploiting big-woods rut patterns is figuring out when a big buck will scent-check a particular doe family group. If you're reading this chapter in the hopes I'll provide a shortcut to success, you can stop now. I haven't figured it out. This is yet one more example where patience is never more of a virtue than when bowhunting big timber. No one can accurately predict where a mature white-tailed buck will be at any given

The author often takes a quick walk-around in his hunting areas to see which hidden runways hold the most fresh sign of big bucks.

moment during the rut. But bowhunting as much as possible near family groups keeps me in the game more than any other rut-hunting strategy I've tried.

Even so, I won't discourage any bowhunter from waiting in ambush along hidden runways during the rut. I probably use that strategy as much as any big-woods bowhunter, but I prefer to hunt around family groups. Why? For one, I've had a bit more success with this strategy. Second, I see more deer, which works wonders for my mental state. Even though I'm not targeting those deer, seeing does, fawns and immature bucks boosts my morale, reminding me it's just a matter of time before a big boy appears.

But there's a downside to sitting where antlerless deer parade by. I've been picked off in my tree stands far more often by antlerless deer than by big bucks. Besides dealing with more pairs of eyes, you're also dealing with more ears and, most notably, more noses. When I know I'll be hunting amid antlerless deer, I take extra precautions. For starters, I make darned sure the trees holding my portable stands have good background cover. And if needed, I place my stands higher than normal.

The toughest part of hunting around antlerless deer is being betrayed by our own odors. This usually isn't difficult to overcome if you're hunting where deer just walk by. It's a different story, however, when setting up where they feed. One of my best big-woods bow-kills came on a large oak flat. The area produced a bumper crop of acorns that year and that oak flat drew lots of hungry deer. I spent most of an entire week trying to get positioned where I could avoid detection by the many does, fawns and small bucks feeding there.

After getting busted a couple of times, I finally found the perfect tree: a large, tri-trunked oak near the east edge of the flat. The tree provided ample cover, and because autumn winds are mostly from the west/northwest where I bowhunt, I didn't worry whether feeding deer would smell me. The mature buck I'd been chasing finally walked within bow range on a frosty morning in early November. He sauntered into the oaks 75 yards away and, true to rutting-buck fashion, began a classic scent-checking routine. I let him close to within 15 yards before putting an arrow through his vitals.

When rutting bucks don't detect estrous scents at their current checkpoint, they quickly move on to check other areas with antlerless deer activity.

165

No one can accurately predict where a mature white-tailed buck will turn up at any given moment during the rut.

Hunting around deer family groups can be a tricky deal because you're often dealing with many sets of eyes, ears and noses.

I also spend plenty of time during the rut bowhunting the downwind sides of doe/fawn bedding areas. As they do with feeding areas, rutting bucks occasionally cruise downwind of these areas to nose-scan for estrous does. The trick is to set up close enough to the bedding area to be within bow range of big bucks that show up, yet still be far enough away to get in and out of your stand without spooking bedded deer. Pulling off this feat requires finding these sites and then learning that magical distance to place your stand. Solving such situations is easier said than done, and each requires a careful approach. Move in, look around, and trust your "feel" and common sense, but don't be surprised if you learn the right distance only through trial and error.

CHAPTER THIRTEEN

MORE FOREST RUT TACTICS

I n the previous chapter we discussed the nomadic movements of big-woods bucks during the rut. Their wanderings can generate the season's most intense excitement when they pass through your area, but just as quickly these bucks can leave you bored and frustrated while chasing does elsewhere in the forest.

When your hopes run high, as they're wont to do during the rut, it's tempting to give up too quickly on a stand and go off in search of better action. Make such decisions carefully. Patience is by far your biggest ally when bowhunting the big-woods rut. Rather than bouncing from one stand to another, it's always best to concentrate your efforts on one or two stands.

Perhaps one of the biggest mistakes you can make is to climb down two hours after sunrise and start poking around. Contrary to what you might have experienced earlier in the season, the first hour and last hour of daylight are not peak activity times for big-timber bucks, at least not during the rut. That isn't just my opinion. In the late 1990s, I started asking hunters attending my seminars for their input on peak-activity times. I also asked dozens of successful bowhunters what time they scored on their bucks. In addition, I kept a running tab on the time of day my hunting partners and I encountered mature bucks during the rut. Those encounters include sightings, close calls and actual kills of mature bucks.

My "research" covered more than 200 sightings of mature, rutting bucks. I was amazed to realize more than 60 percent of those encounters occurred between 9 a.m. and 3 p.m. Obviously, the midday hours are the most productive time to bowhunt mature bucks during the rut. In fact, the percentage of midday big-buck

Contrary to what we often hear, the first hour and last hour of daylight are not peak activity times for big bucks. At least not during the rut.

During the rut, big bucks move whenever they get the urge. This could just as likely be noon as midnight.

sightings would be even higher if more bowhunters stayed in their tree stands during those hours. I know several consistently successful bowhunters who don't enter the woods until an hour or two after daylight. They've learned big-buck activity increases as the day wears on, and they see no need to hurry out of bed each morning. Given their success rates, I can't argue with them.

A few seasons ago I had back-to-back run-ins with two big bucks while bowhunting a forested area near home. The first buck, a huge-bodied 150-class 10-pointer, sauntered into view at 1:45 p.m. He was trailing an estrous doe and walked within 30 yards of my tree stand. Unfortunately, I had my 20-yard sight pin on him instead of my 30-yard pin when I released the arrow. I returned to the stand before dawn the next day in hopes of getting a second chance. He didn't show up, but about 11:30 a.m. a different 10-pointer appeared. Again, the distance was about 30 yards, and again I executed a clean miss!

Those two incidents don't say much for my shooting skills, but they speak volumes about the potential for seeing big bucks at midday. Just to reinforce that point, and to show I don't always miss, I arrowed a 10-pointer at 9:30 a.m. in 1998, and the next year I ambushed a 7-point, 204-pound (field dressed) buck at 2:30 p.m.

RATTLING DURING THE RUT

No matter what time of day you hunt, take my advice and never leave home without your rattling antlers. Although rattling is usually not as effective during the rut as the pre-rut, it's effective enough during a big-woods hunt to justify carrying antlers or a rattling bag at all times. Never forget, though, that the secret to rattling during the rut is location, location, location. Although some bowhunters always think they can rattle up bucks anywhere they stop in the forest, this tactic is seldom a matter of just banging two antlers together.

Although I've had good success rattling in bucks, please realize my description of "good success" is a response rate of about 5 percent. In other words, 95 times out of 100 I detect no response to my efforts. But hey, I'm a realist, and see nothing wrong with those numbers. Unfortunately, most bowhunters head into the woods thinking those numbers should be reversed. Maybe they hold that belief because rattling always seems to work on deer hunting

171

videos and TV shows. Be assured, videos and TV shows would be 20 times longer if they showed every unsuccessful rattling session!

Remember, too, that many of those videotaped rattling sessions occur on private ranches in Texas, which can be an entirely different world of deer hunting. Most Texas ranches shown on TV are professionally managed, and they have nearly even buck-to-doe ratios. As a result, they have excellent numbers of mature bucks ready to challenge each other for breeding rights. Such places are a rattler's paradise.

Even though buck-to-doe ratios are often excellent in forests and the deep woods, don't forget that deer densities are often low. That means there just aren't many deer running around, let alone mature bucks. The few mature bucks roaming big timber are seemingly scattered across the forest, and so your best rattling efforts are seldom heard by a mature buck. On the other hand, when a big buck is within hearing range, it will usually check out "the fights." You must continue to rattle no matter how many times it fails, because you never know when your luck will turn.

Even so, save your rattling for places where it's most likely to work. Never forget that mature bucks won't charge into areas where they don't feel comfortable. One of my favorite areas for rattling is near feeding areas used by antlerless deer. Big bucks know adult does would blow the whistle if things weren't safe, and will enter these sites braced for action. That's another reason I like to rattle near antlerless feeding areas: I believe big bucks respond aggressively at these sites because they think the fight they hear must concern a hot doe. Judging by their body language when they respond to rattling, I believe these mature bucks are expecting to "get sideways" in an all-out brawl.

Another likely rattling site during the rut is along hidden runways, especially those with big, fresh rubs. When I hunt along hidden runways, I enter my stand some time during the morning, stay put all day, and rattle fairly often.

What do I mean by "fairly often?" During the rut, I rattle three times each hour. When I'm not rattling, I keep my eyes and ears open for anything that might indicate a big buck is nearby. Not only that, but if I spot a big buck or think I hear one, I'm rattling now! How long are my rattling sequences? No two sequences are the same length, but I never rattle less than 30 seconds and never

Many hunters head into the woods believing they should be able to rattle in a buck every time they smash their antlers together.

173

more than 90 seconds. Of course, I quit rattling immediately if I see or hear a buck approaching.

One important caution about rattling: Although the temptation is tremendous, never rattle when your stand is within open view of a big buck. When a buck hears rattling, it immediately achieves visual lock-on to the sounds. What do you suppose the buck thinks when he can't see the combatants even though he has a clear view of where they should be? I believe that's the most common and most costly mistake hunters make when trying to rattle in big bucks. If you don't think mature bucks can figure out such situations with rudimentary reasoning, you might want to re-evaluate your own reasoning powers.

I've rattled and grunted in enough mature bucks to know they don't require additional calling to pinpoint the sounds. I've called in several big-woods bucks that covered great distances and still pinpointed the calling source right down to my very tree! In none of these instances did I do any additional calling to help them out.

DECOYS DO WORK!

I've had a ton of experience using decoys in farm country during the rut, but I've had little experience using them in forests and deep woods. Even so, those few experiences convinced me decoys can be effective in the big woods.

No matter where you use decoys, the vital key in luring big bucks to your setup is making sure your decoy is placed where it can be seen from far away. Although that requirement is more easily satisfied in farm country, it can be accomplished in the big woods. One such setting is first-year clearcuts. In fact, these clearcuts are probably the best place of all for decoying in the big woods because of long-range visibility. In addition, rutting bucks spend a lot of time around these clearcuts. As a result, you stand a good chance of seeing some big buck/decoy interactions.

The edges of grassy swamps are also great places for decoys during the rut, because bucks seem to relate to these areas during the rut. Why? These swamps often provide bedding sites for antlerless deer. How can bucks see your decoy in swamp grasses that stand as high as deer? It takes only a few minutes to remedy the situation. I simply stomp the grass flat in about a 10- to 15-yard radius, and then place my decoy in the middle of the new clearing. It's amaz-

During the rut, the author tries to rattle at every big buck he sees or hears.

In the right situations, decoys can be effective tools for duping big-woods bucks. Recent clearcuts are probably your best bet for these setups.

ing how much difference this makes. Rather than being nearly hidden in the grass, the decoy stands out like a pimple on your nose.

Obviously, there's more to decoying than just plunking them down and climbing into your stand. For instance, not just any decoy works for big bucks. After my first 10 years of decoying experience, I decided a buck decoy is always the best choice. Judging by what I've seen, buck decoys consistently attract more mature bucks than do doe decoys.

In addition, always place your decoy upwind from your stand, and keep it within bow range. Just don't overdo it. Put it far enough away so there's room for bucks to walk between the decoy and your stand. Also, be sure it faces the right way. It's this simple: Buck decoys should face you and doe decoys should face away. Why? Because bucks usually approach another buck head-on,

Always place your decoy within a distance you feel confident shooting your bow. But don't overdo it. Leave room for a buck to walk between your stand and the decoy.

and they usually approach does from behind to sniff their rump.

I've pinpointed two specific periods when big bucks are most likely to approach a decoy: the late pre-rut and the rut. That doesn't mean decoys never work at other times. They sometimes do, but the late pre-rut and the rut are, without doubt, prime decoy time.

FUNNELS CAN BE PRODUCTIVE

Another great way to slay rutting bucks is to set up in funnels. I can't think of a better time than the peak of the rut to set up such ambushes, Although hidden runways can be productive during the big-woods rut, I've found funnel hunting equally productive at this time. Granted, some big bucks are already with does, but have confidence that there's a few frustrated "bachelors" running around. Those bucks will be cruising nearly 24/7. The trick is spending your time in funnels that attract the most big-buck travels.

Just as they're used to evaluate hidden runways, rub sign can also help you judge the potential of funnels. Funnels with lots of rub sign obviously channel more buck activity than do funnels with few rubs. That doesn't mean you should turn your back on funnels with little buck sign. Here's the deal: Some big-woods funnels are slow almost all autumn before becoming hot hubs of buck action during the rut. The best funnels, almost without exception, are found between two antlerless-deer activity areas.

Those areas might be a half-mile or mile apart, and rutting bucks often walk through the same funnels time and again. However, they don't always make rubs and scrapes in these funnels. This is yet one more example of why you must have an intimate understanding of the forest or deep woods you're hunting. Knowing exactly where does and fawns bed and/or feed can pay dividends once the rut kicks into gear. Dig out your topo maps and aerial photos and look for funnels between those antlerless activity areas. I can almost assure you that, at least during the rut, these will be the hottest of all funnels.

Before closing I'll reiterate the importance of spending at least a few days during the rut hunting your favorite stands at midday. Those who have never tried it will find it difficult to spend lunch time in the woods, but I'm confident it will take only one or two midday hunts to convince you big bucks couldn't care less about time of day when the rut is in full swing.

178

Much as they're used to reveal and evaluate hidden runways in the forest, rubs can also be used to evaluate the potential of funnel areas.

CHAPTER FOURTEEN

LATE SEASON IN THE DEEP WOODS

I wish I could say I've enjoyed great success bowhunting forests and deep woods during the late season. Unfortunately, I haven't, but it's not for lack of trying. I'm sure I've spent as many cold, lonely hours on late-season bow stands as anyone in the North Woods.

If I've learned one thing from my late-season bowhunts, it's that they're one of the big woods' toughest gigs. I'm not alone, either. I've talked to dozens of big-woods bowhunters who share my views. Almost to a man they dread returning to the late-season woods, but that doesn't mean they throw in the towel. And I don't either. It's just one more unexplainable challenge that keeps us caught up in this sport.

WHY THE LATE SEASON IS TOUGH

One of the biggest challenges facing big-woods bowhunters in the late season is the scarcity of deer. This situation is tough enough during the early archery season, but in most forests and deep woods it becomes even more frustrating in the late season. I think the biggest reason is that these final weeks of bow season follow the gun season. Not only are fewer deer roaming the forest than before, but the number of mature bucks is certainly lower.

Many forests I've hunted had no surplus of trophy-class bucks to start with, and the few that remain in the late season are more scattered than before. Although you might find small pockets of does, fawns and immature bucks, you'll seldom find mature bucks hanging out together. With few exceptions, mature bucks

180

Bowhunting's many challenges help explain why we get so caught up in this sport year after year.

At no other time during archery season are mature deer as flighty, suspicious and nocturnal in their behavior as they are during late fall and early winter.

live in solitude during the late season. In addition, their temperament changes. At no other time in archery season are mature bucks as flighty, suspicious and nocturnal in behavior as they are during the late season.

The cumulative effects of hunting pressure put them into full-scale survival mode. These big bucks put up with at least a month of skulking bowhunters. Then came the invading hordes of blaze orange-clad gun-hunters. Mature whitetails tolerate only so much poking, prodding and maybe even shooting before they hunker down into an impenetrable lair. Once they're in this survival mode, they cling to low-profile behaviors long after gun hunters depart. Unfortunately, they remain in that mode when archers get their final chances to fill their tags.

For obvious reasons, this is also when familiarity with your hunting areas proves most beneficial. If you don't already know vital information about the land, I can almost guarantee you'll spin your wheels in the late season.

KNOW WHERE BIG BUCKS BED

I mentioned earlier that mature bucks adopt fairly nocturnal lifestyles during the late season. Notice I said fairly, not totally. I believe most mature bucks move a little in daylight, even during the late season. Why then do so many late-season bowhunters believe big bucks are "totally nocturnal?" I think it's because most of them set up where no big buck would ever appear in daylight late in the year, leaving unfortunate bowhunters to conclude the bucks are nocturnal.

I've spent a lot of time the past 20 years bowhunting the late season, some of it in farm country and some in forests. One important fact remains constant, regardless of the environment: Rarely have I seen big bucks moving around far from their bedding areas in daylight. Based on my experiences, it would be easy to assume big bucks go totally nocturnal in the late season. But because I've dedicated many hours to pinpointing their bedding areas, I know better. The key to seeing them in daylight is placing your stands as close as possible to where they bed. Not surprisingly, the best time to pinpoint those spots is during post-season and spring scouting missions.

The importance of setting up on their doorstep became clear

to me on a late-afternoon bowhunt years ago on a brutally cold mid-December day in northwestern Wisconsin. The hunt's first 90 minutes slipped by without incident, but soon after the sun sank below the horizon I heard a slight rustling in a nearby tamarack swamp. Several seconds later a monster buck walked out. The buck went a few steps into the hardwoods flat where I sat, and then stopped to scan the area.

I thought the buck was mine. He was about 50 yards away and seemed unaware of me. About 20 minutes of hunting light remained, and he only had to move another 20 yards to be within range. It seemed inevitable the buck would follow the rub line my stand overlooked. Five minutes went by, and then 10. The buck moved only his head and ears the entire time. Five more minutes passed, but now he gave no indication he would continue my way. Talk about a standoff! The final minutes of legal hunting time ticked away, and the 10-pointer still stood where he had first stopped. With daylight gone, I could only slide my bow onto its hanger and watch as darkness swallowed the trophy whitetail. Just before the forest turned black, the buck slowly walked back into the swamp, never appearing the least bit alarmed.

What made this experience especially bitter was that I had originally considered setting up closer to the swamp. Had I done so, the buck would have been standing 10 yards away! Don't ask why I backed off to my actual site, because I don't know. It just seemed the better choice at the time.

In the years since that encounter, I've seen several other big bucks do nearly the same thing. They all walked into view with plenty of light remaining, but then hung up near the edge of their sanctuaries. They always stood in one spot, constantly sniffing the air and studying their surroundings until darkness closed in. Those experiences highlight the importance of setting up near the edges of big-buck bedding areas. Remember, we're bowhunting. Being a few yards out of position is often the difference between joy and frustration.

Your best chances for big-buck action on morning hunts also require hunting near the edges of bedding areas. Because of their skittish late-season behavior, big bucks usually leave feeding areas before the first traces of light. That means that they'll be

The author believes big bucks seldom become totally nocturnal. They might not wander far or often in daylight, but move they do.

near their bedding areas by the time daylight penetrates the forest. It also means you must get up extra early and make long walks through dark woods. You'll probably need to figure out routes that let you bypass areas where you're likely to bump into deer. Once at your stand, you must be ready for action as soon as it's light enough to see. Rarely do big bucks in the late season continue moving well into the morning.

If you've done your homework, you should have a good idea where bucks leave and enter their bedding areas. Much as they did during the pre-rut, bucks now follow their rub lines, often reworking some rubs and making new ones. Use this evidence to pinpoint which rub lines have the most potential. Never forget these are routes that make big bucks feel the most safe and secure. Then again, even minor human activity makes bucks alter their routines during the late season. It's essential you keep your presence as secret as possible. After all, even if you're extra careful, the best you can hope for is one chance at a mature buck. Anything less than your best effort won't produce even that!

WHEN IT'S OK TO HUNT NEAR FOOD

Certain late-season situations, of course, warrant setups near or inside feeding areas. Those circumstances always involve weather. In the North Woods, heavy snows and/or brutal cold can prompt mature bucks to forsake caution. Therefore, setups near food sources during heavy snowfalls can be productive. In fact, deer activity is more intense in the hours preceding major winter storms. Whitetails — and all animals, for that matter — sense major weather systems many hours before they arrive. As a result, deer go on eating binges, especially in advance of major snowfalls.

Which foods deer target depends on the area. In my region their main early-winter foods are woody browse and buds, so I focus my bowhunts in and around recently logged areas. In fact, ongoing logging activity often creates red-hot action. I've seen deer, including some huge bucks, flock to such places even as loggers work, especially when temperatures are brutal for several days. Whitetails must keep their bellies full of nutritious foods in those conditions to maintain their energy

The author has often watched individual bucks standing in one spot at dusk, sniffing the air currents and studying their surroundings. And that's where they remained when darkness settled in.

187

White-tailed bucks often make fresh rubs and rework some of their old rubs during the late season.

The author is not a big believer in the so-called second rut. Experience taught him there's a world of difference between a full-blown rut and isolated cases of late-season breeding activity.

reserves. However, it's a balancing act. To avoid burning excess energy, they prefer the discarded tops of freshly felled trees, which are loaded with high-energy, easily digested browse. In my region, this means buds and tender twigs from poplar, birch and maples; as well as cedar and hemlock fronds. It's also crucial they not work hard to get the food. To conserve energy, they follow well-packed trails to reach logging sites, and then

189

Observations of individual deer movements can provide key information during the late season. Watch freshly logged sites and other feeding areas from a distance to pinpoint prime stand sites.

patiently eat everything within reach before walking to other fallen treetops.

As with any large feeding area, it can be difficult to figure out where deer are keying their activity. Snow cover, of course, can be a huge help in determining where to place your stands. Even then you could be slightly out of position. Is there a quick fix? You bet. Direct observations are even more important now than they were earlier in the season, because deer are fewer and they're skittish. You must position your stands in the right spots as quickly as possible. Of course, you could take a chance and choose your spot based entirely on sign. However, I suggest placing a portable tree stand a safe distance from activity areas and then watching those sites the last few hours of daylight.

Don't rush this process. It might take more than one day of watching to figure out what's going on, so be patient. You might get only one chance to capitalize on your findings. Therefore, it's worth the time and effort to assemble all the puzzle pieces before moving in to hunt. Also remember to "map" antlerless activity. Your objective is finding sites within bow range of big bucks, but you must also know how does and fawns use those areas. You don't want to get busted by some loud-mouthed doe or fawn before a big buck walks into range.

WHAT ABOUT THE SECOND RUT?

OK, so what about the so-called second rut? Is there such a thing? And if so, is it possible to take advantage of it? Let me say this: You'll be disappointed if you go into the late season depending on the second rut to pull a big buck into bow range. I'm not saying breeding is nonexistent during the late season. Judging by late fawn births each summer, some breeding obviously occurs late in the year. But there's a huge difference between isolated breeding encounters and a full-blown rut.

By the time a bowhunter realizes breeding activity is under way in the late season, it's almost too late to act. Sometimes, though, you can squeeze out one more shooting opportunity by rattling and grunt-calling while breeding activity is under way or immediately after it ends. After all, you can almost guarantee one or more bucks missed out on this final chance to breed, leaving themselves vulnerable to rattling and grunting. The key to success is to make sure you rattle and call from the heart of the site where the breeding occurred. That's where the bucks that lost out on the action will be hanging out. They'll think the renewed fight or the tending grunts mean the breeding action has resumed.

ONE AND DONE?

No matter how you arrange a shooting opportunity in the late season, realize it will likely be your only chance. I can't believe how many "one-timers" I've had over the years. One in particular still haunts me. The buck was a heavy-horned 10-pointer I started chasing during the early archery season. Unlike most mature big-woods bucks I've hunted, this stud stayed visible. I saw him three times during the archery season and once during Wisconsin's nine-day firearms season. To say this buck led a charmed life would be an understatement. As I learned during the late season, he was charmed beyond belief.

On the final day of our state's late archery season, New Year's Eve, the temperature was a horribly cold 20 degrees below zero when I left my cabin. At about 4:30 p.m., after I'd been on stand for 90 minutes, the deer I'd been chasing nearly three months reappeared. The trophy buck soon cut the distance to 13 steps, and then stopped to browse. My bow was in my hands, and all I had to do was pull the arrow to full draw. Unfortunately, the buck faced me almost head-on.

I just waited and hoped, but I froze out before he offered a shot. I finally had to concede defeat, so I scared him away and hung up my bow. Then I warmed my hands just enough to safely climb down. I was on the ground gathering my gear when I got the feeling I was being watched. Turning, I saw the buck about 50 yards away. For some reason he had returned and was watching me. I was a bit shocked, but then I felt disappointment and, finally, respect. I had hunted the buck long and hard, but he had beaten me at every turn.

I left the woods, taking comfort there would be other seasons and other days for that big-woods buck.

At about 4:30 p.m. on Dec. 31 one year — the final day of the late archery season — a buck the author had been chasing nearly three months finally appeared within bow range.

CHAPTER FIFTEEN

THE HUNTER'S SIXTH SENSE

I feel obligated to warn you that this chapter contains some of the most controversial ideas you've probably ever read about bowhunting trophy whitetails. I'm convinced, however, that my ideas about our "sixth sense" or inner voice are worth discussing because they've made a huge difference during many of my big-woods bowhunts.

I also stress that almost all hunters possess a sixth sense to some degree, even though some of us are more attuned to hunches, instincts and unexplained perceptions. In fact, I believe in my sixth sense almost as much as my senses of sight, hearing, touch, smell and taste. I recall the first time I realized I should pay attention to my intuition. The experience took place on a big-woods gun-hunt during the mid-1970s. I was on a stand atop a slight ridge, watching a hardwoods hillside that dropped to a flat about 75 yards wide. At its far side the flat abutted a clearcut in its third year of regrowth.

My brother Mike had killed a buck at this spot the previous year, but he was now hunting a stand near a second-year clearcut several miles away. Mike suggested I hunt his old spot at least one day during the gun season. He didn't need to twist my arm. I knew it was a good idea. I spent several hours the weekend before gun season scouting the area. Judging by the sign, deer were using the same trails and doing much the same things as the year before, so I decided I couldn't improve on Mike's choice in stand sites.

Shortly after daylight on opening day, my sixth sense kicked in. For some reason, my attention kept returning to a spot 75 yards south of the stand. I didn't understand why. The spot had

The author believes most bowhunters have a sixth sense that often helps them in the deer woods. Still, some individuals trust this sense much more than others do.

not piqued my interest while scouting the previous weekend. In fact, I hadn't found any trails, rubs, scrapes, tracks or other sign that indicated I should expect a buck to show up there. Even so, I found myself continually looking at the spot, and each time I looked, my sense of anticipation grew stronger.

About an hour after daylight, with my attention again drawn to the spot, I got the shock of my life. A big buck was standing exactly where I had been looking! Somehow, the buck had slipped within 75 yards of me without making a noise. The big 8-pointer's sudden appearance generated an instant case of buck fever. Even though my knees shook uncontrollably, I somehow made an accurate shot as the buck moved slowly through the hardwoods flat. He then ran a short distance and tipped over. Not until I stood over my trophy and admired him did I remember the feeling I'd had before he appeared. What made me keep looking at the spot where he eventually appeared?

One of my hunting partners was on a stand nearby that morning. Soon after I shot, he walked over to see if I had killed a buck. I remember trying to decide whether to tell him about that unexplainable feeling, but decided it was a fluke and not worth mentioning. The next year I had to re-evaluate my conclusion. I was bowhunting the first week of bow season when the weird feeling returned. Again I was sneaking looks at a specific spot near my stand. And also like the previous year, I had scouted the area enough to know the spot didn't appear "deer-friendly." As I sat there, I figured I was subconsciously trying to re-create what had happened the previous year.

But then I started getting little adrenaline rushes whenever I looked at the spot. The "rushes" resembled the feelings I get when a buck walks into view, and on the umpteenth time I looked at the spot, that's what happened! A young 6-point buck with a small rack walked into view just as my eyes came into focus, and then stopped at the spot I had repeatedly eye-balled the past hour. Granted, I didn't want to shoot this buck, but I couldn't deny I had somehow known it would appear on that exact spot. This felt more than eerie!

Even though I could no longer deny the feeling, I now had a problem: I felt I must tell my friends about it. Over supper that night at our North Woods cabin, I told my hunting partners

The author remembers the first time he noticed his sixth sense at work. His attention was continually drawn to the exact spot where a big 8-point buck eventually appeared.

Have you ever "heard" an inner voice that tells you to look behind you, or to hang a stand in a spot that doesn't intrigue most bowhunters? If the author had never experienced such feelings himself, he doubts he would believe someone else's claims of unexplained hunches.

about my two experiences with the feeling. I was about half-way through my story about the buck from the previous year when the looks on everyone's faces told me to stop. They didn't believe a word. In looking back, I don't blame them for their skepticism. Had I never experienced the feeling, I doubt I would have believed someone else's claim of having a sixth sense.

That's the way it seems to go with this thing. Trying to explain it to someone who has never felt it is like describing the color blue to someone born blind. It simply can't be done.

WHY A SIXTH SENSE IS INVALUABLE

As we've discussed, big-timber bowhunters face a huge task in trying to learn everything possible about deer roaming their area. We must learn where they bed and feed, and where they walk when traveling between the two places. We also must try to figure out the bucks' size, even though we seldom see them beforehand to help us gauge and pattern them. And regardless of how good you might be at reading and deciphering buck sign, you still must speculate a bit when patterning them. That's where the sixth sense can be invaluable.

I can't help but recall some thoughts from this book's editor, Patrick Durkin, when we were outlining chapter ideas via e-mail. As he wrote: "It's never more important to trust your instincts than when hunting the big woods. Sometimes it's a special feeling about a particular site no one else pauses to examine. Other times it's listening to an inner voice that tells you to turn and look behind you even when there was no tell-tale sound to alert you."

Bingo! That's the best way I can describe how the hunter's sixth sense works. Dozens of times while bowhunting the big woods I've gravitated toward a spot simply because of some subconscious pull — a pull I've learned not to resist. On almost every occasion, the spot that attracted me was the focus of big-buck activity. And, as I've written, I've often heard an inner voice that warns me a deer will show up in a particular spot. That same voice has also warned me of big whitetails trying to sneak behind me.

Even though I believe most bowhunters have a special sixth sense, I also believe most of them usually ignore it, even if unintentionally. Most hunters simply don't recognize the feeling when it surfaces. For instance, I once ran a deer hunting con-

199

In almost every instance where the author found himself drawn to a spot while scouting, his examination revealed that it attracted lots of big-buck activity.

sulting business that assisted hunters in learning more about their lands. I studied topo maps and aerials photos of the land and walked as much of it as possible. Along the way I would point out to my client how he could better hunt his property.

I worked with many hunters during that five-year period, and almost all of them displayed a sixth sense. Even so, each and every one of them failed to put it to use. I would often notice them looking toward a distant spot, one that I also wanted to check, probably because I had also gotten a feeling about it. Instead of heading toward the spot, however, they invariably turned and walked elsewhere. This happened several times before I asked why they turned their backs on a spot that piqued their curiosity. One guy's answer spoke for all: "Yeah, I had a feeling something might be going on, but I didn't think it was worth walking over to check."

Even those who trust their instincts developed their faith over time. They might have ignored the feelings at first, but then started compiling positive results when following their instincts.

Bowhunters who trust gut feelings usually had to learn to follow their instincts. In most cases, they experienced positive results when listening to their inner voice.

As a result, when the feeling tells them to look more closely at a distant spot, you can bet they'll check it out!

VENISON BALONEY?

By now some of you better understand why I opened this chapter by warning it could be controversial. If you think this sixth-sense stuff is a bunch of venison baloney, you might want to move on to the next chapter. But I think most hunters can relate to what I'm talking about, even though most of us seldom share such insights with other hunters! In most cases, we've learned it's best to keep our mouths shut, especially when we're tempted to share premonitions about where a buck will appear. I know some bowhunters think I'm wasting their time when I try discussing it with them.

Let's be clear about a few things, though: I'll never claim anyone can make a deer appear at their beck and call. Nor do I know when "feelings" will come to me. In fact, I've had intense feelings a deer would show up, but then nothing happened. Why, I don't know. Finally, I also can't predict whether a doe, buck or fawn will show up after I get those feelings. Maybe other hunters can, but I can't.

OTHER WAYS TO USE YOUR SIXTH SENSE

Another way your sixth sense can help is when you find yourself wondering if you're putting too much pressure on a stand site. That gut feeling is your sixth sense telling you that you've worn out your welcome on the spot. Overhunting a stand, especially one that might have great potential later in the season, is the biggest mistake a big-woods hunter can make. Productive stand sites can be rare in the big woods, so take every precaution to ensure you don't spoil such hotspots. If your gut says you might be overdoing it, you probably are. Back off and let the area rest for four or five days before trying again.

One of the most intense feelings I've ever had in the big timber occurred years ago while hunting a specific buck most of the season. Because I had been pressuring the buck for several days, I decided to give him a rest on a cool November afternoon. After thinking it over, I decided to hunt an area about 10 miles from where the buck lived. But then as I drove down a state highway to carry out my plan, a feeling shot through me like an electrical jolt. I whipped a U-turn and headed back toward the buck's

In many cases, a few flickers of movement give the author enough information to make him confident he knows whether an approaching deer will be a buck or doe.

stomping grounds. About 25 minutes later I was atop a portable tree stand near the brute's bedding area. The buck walked past an hour later and, as the saying goes, he was soon history.

I could recall several more experiences where my sixth sense helped tag a big-woods buck, but you've got the picture. I'll close this chapter by predicting you'll experience many situations when all you can do is follow a hunch, gut-feeling, premonition or an inner voice. No matter what you call the feeling, when it tries to get your attention, remember what you read in this chapter. You're not crazy. You're just tuned in.

203

CHAPTER SIXTEEN

GETTING YOUR DEER OUT

Not every challenge we face when bowhunting whitetails in forests and deep woods revolves around the deer themselves. For instance, one could argue that our primary challenge is taking care to ensure we get ourselves out of the woods each night! We must always know our whereabouts and constantly keep our bearings when chasing wilderness whitetails. After all, spending an unplanned night in the forest is never pleasant, no matter how well-equipped we might be to handle an emergency.

When you walk into the forest each morning, never assume you'll remain within easy reach of where you're parked or camped. For instance, if you make a marginal hit and must track a buck deep into the forest, bowhunting's code of ethics requires that you see the job to its end. And although I wrote an entire chapter detailing why deeper isn't always better when bowhunting the big woods, there will be times when you must hunt far from the nearest road if you hope to score. That means you'll do far more legwork when bowhunting forests and deep woods than you'll ever do in other environments.

As if that's not enough to discourage a few aspiring big-woods bowhunters, let's not overlook one of the "rewards" if you kill a monster buck: How do you get him out of the woods when you're a mile or more from the road, trail or path? And even if you have the individual or team strength to pull him out, how do you avoid dragging all the hair off his hide?

IT WASN'T ALWAYS EASY!

I've always liked my father's story about an ordeal he and my

You dropped your big-woods trophy a mile from the nearest road. Now the real work begins: getting your deer out of the forest.

This is the way many hunters get their deer back to civilization, but it requires lots of hard work and can damage your trophy's cape.

Uncle Clayton experienced with one of their bucks. As was habit in their early big-woods days during the mid-1950s, Dad and Uncle Clayton were poking around "way back in" when one of them shot a big buck at midmorning.

Another member of their party heard the shots and found Dad and Clayton just as they started the long drag. The fellow generously offered to carry their rifles and then told them, "I'll go ahead a ways and wait, and then I'll take a turn dragging that ol' buck."

Dad and Uncle Clayton watched their partner walk off and disappear into the forest. Little did they know that was the last they'd see of him until they reached camp that evening. "We dragged that big buck for close to an hour before it dawned on us that our buddy hadn't waited as promised," Dad told me years later. To say Dad and Uncle Clayton were miffed would be an understatement. Of course, time helped ease their bitterness, and both now laugh when recalling the story.

"At first, Clayton and I thought maybe he had continued on to the road and headed to camp for some help," Dad said. In reality, the guy never intended to help them drag the buck or recruit more help. As Dad and Uncle Clayton soon learned, their "partner" had simply taken their guns and walked away as a joke. Realize, too, this was no quarter-mile drag. It was a deep-woods marathon event. Dad recalled: "By the time we got that buck out to the road we had dragged just about all the hair off both sides up to the middle of its neck. We couldn't even think about getting it mounted."

GETTING THEM OUT INTACT

Obviously, we have more ways today than ever to make such jobs less taxing, but not everyone chooses to use the new methods. Maybe some of us are just stubborn in refusing to deviate from "the old ways." In fact, until about 15 years ago, my partners and I knew only one hauling method. We tied a rope around the antlers and dragged our bucks out of the forest, just as my dad and his hunting partners had done the previous 50 years.

Since then we've had to acknowledge dramatic improvements in hauling out deer, and I'm not just talking about ATVs. As my hunting partners and I learned, even ATVs can't go everywhere.

207

When ATVs became popular in recent years, getting a deer out of the forest became much simpler. Just be sure it's legal to use them when you're hunting public lands. Some public forests don't allow ATVs or restrict them to specific hours and tasks.

As a result, we've found alternative methods we like, especially if the dead buck has a field-dressed weight exceeding 200 pounds! Body weight isn't the only factor we consider, though. If a big-woods buck deserves a place on the wall, it's imperative we protect the cape during the trip out, which is no small duty.

I usually use one of three methods to get big bucks out of the forest without ruining the hide. Not only that, but none requires enormous energy. The first method costs less than $20, and is a

Big-woods trophies like this deserve special treatment. Innovative bowhunters have several tested ways to get big bucks out of the woods with little investments of time, effort and/or money.

209

Two-wheel carts like this can serve a couple of purposes. They can be used to haul deer out of the woods or to carry your gear deep into the woods with little effort.

prized toy of every kid living near a hill in snow country. Hey, a plastic sled can be a lifesaver for sliding deer out of the woods, whether there's snow cover or not!

Keep a few things in mind, however, when using a plastic sled. First, replace its thin tow rope that comes as standard equipment. Not only will these factory-installed ropes cut harshly into your hands when hauling out a big buck, they'll also break — repeatedly. In addition, bring along several 2- to 3-foot lengths of thinner rope for tying off your trophy's legs and head to keep them from hooking trees, branches, logs and underbrush as you skid them from the woods. Few things are as frustrating as continually stopping to free antlers and/or legs from obstacles along your route.

An alternative to a plastic sled is the plastic tarp. I've often used these inexpensive tarps and found they make the drag much easier. I just wrap the deer inside the tarp, tie up the package with a heavy rope, and tie a 4-foot rope to the buck's antlers. I then tie that rope to a wrist-thick stick that's 14 to 16 inches long. The stick, which I cut at the scene, serves as my dragging

A deer cart with two wheels and a low center of gravity is the best design. Covering your deer can protect it from dirt and flies during transport.

handle. One vital caution: Take the deer out of the tarp as soon as you reach the road, lay it on its back, and prop open the body cavity with a stout stick. Carcasses that aren't properly cooled can quickly spoil, costing you the cape and valuable table fare.

Another effective method for getting deer to your vehicle involves the increasingly popular two-wheel carts. Although one person can usually handle a deer cart, two people make the job almost enjoyable. Everyone who uses these carts raves about them, and never again drags out deer the old-fashioned way.

My good friend and the editor of this book, Patrick Durkin, even used a homemade rickshaw for many years when hunting northwestern Ontario, northern Wisconsin and Michigan's Upper Peninsula. He told me the cart proved its worth every time he pulled it out of his truck. "Two-wheeled carts work like a charm," he said. "I not only use mine for getting deer out of the woods, but also for hauling in portable tree stands on public land, and lumber and nails for permanent stands on private property where I have permission to hunt."

Durkin built his rickshaw years ago from an old bicycle before deer carts were offered commercially, but he concedes his design doesn't stack up to today's mass-manufactured models. "I'm not an engineer, so my rickshaw is too top-heavy when it's carrying a deer. Commercial carts have a lower center of gravity, so it's almost impossible to tip them over. Mine tipped over a few times and tossed me like a rag doll, but I put up with it. I knew it still beat dragging a deer by the antlers."

When buying or building a cart, stay away from single-wheel models. Not only do they require two people, but it's tough enough trying to maneuver a loaded cart around obstacles without having to also worry about keeping it balanced. Even with two people, single-wheel carts aren't as trouble-free as two-wheel models. No matter how clear your route through the woods, it's still unpaved terrain. You'll need to do some tricky maneuvering and, more than likely, you'll do some lifting to get the cart over logs, rocks and other obstacles. It's much easier to do this if one person lifts the cart while the other "pulls on the yokes."

As with plastic sleds and tarps, lash your deer securely to the cart to ensure the head, antlers and legs don't catch on obstacles along your route. Durkin uses ropes and bungee cords for that

213

It's imperative for those who bowhunt whitetails on public lands to avoid inflicting lasting scars on those lands. Strive to tread lightly whenever possible.

purpose, but says bungees are far superior. A tip: To hook bungees onto your cart with little effort, install screw-eyes in convenient places if your cart isn't so equipped.

FORGET THE POLES!

Maybe you noticed I didn't mention another means of getting deer out of the woods. I'm sure many of you have seen old-time photos of deer lashed to long, stout poles being carried by two hunters. The hunters are smiling from each end of the pole while holding it atop their shoulders, seemingly out for a pleasant stroll. Judging by the many such photos, this must have been a popular way to carry out deer in the "olden days."

But I always wonder how far they actually carried those deer. I've tried this system, and it's the most exhausting and painful experience I've had in the deer woods! To keep the deer from swinging awkwardly, you must stay perfectly in step with your partner on the other end of the pole. In addition, you must stay vigilant in studying the ground in front of you. Otherwise you'll keep stepping into holes, and tripping over logs, rocks, branches, brush and other obstacles. And trust me, you will trip no matter how closely you study the terrain ahead! When you do, you'll become much more aware of that deer-laden pole on your shoulder. It ain't pleasant, believe me!

SUMMARY

I'll end this chapter by stressing a vital point: Depending on where your buck falls, it's pretty much a given you'll need to do a little path clearing to get it out. Whatever you do, minimize the work as much as possible. Whether you hunt whitetails on public or private lands, avoid making lasting disturbances to the habitat.

Maybe that's one reason I'm not an ATV fan. It's virtually impossible to take an ATV off-trail without inflicting scars to the land. To my way of thinking, that's unacceptable. I'm aware that restricting ATV usage to authorized trails means having to bust our butts to some degree when retrieving a big buck. So be it! Those of us who hunt public lands must keep in mind that we don't own the forest. We're merely using it. We owe it to future generations of big-woods bowhunters to leave as few clues to our temporary presence as possible.

215

CHAPTER SEVENTEEN

DEEP-WOODS BOW CAMPS

Many years have come and gone since November 1964 when I first ventured into the big woods, but I still recall those moments as if they were just a few sunrises ago. Some memories, of course, involve specific hunts I made with Dad and my brother Mike.

One such moment is my first big-woods kill. It happened around midday on the second day of the November gun season. That first whitetail didn't carry antlers, but she sure made me proud. I was standing next to Dad, who spotted the deer first. "Don't move, Greg," he whispered. "Here come some deer." I turned toward the direction Dad was looking and spotted three deer approaching. "Wait until they get right in front of us and then shoot the one in front," Dad said. The three deer walked within 15 yards of Dad and me. The Model 94 Winchester was already at my shoulder, and all three deer stopped and looked when I cocked the hammer.

I put the sights on the lead doe's vitals and touched off the .32 Special. The doe dropped in her tracks. I'd never seen anything like that! The next thing I knew Dad was patting me on the back and saying, "Nice shot, Greg!" Then he added, "Walk over and make sure she's down for good, but don't get too close." I remember helping Dad and Mike drag her to our car, which was parked on a logging road. I also recall driving back to camp, hanging my doe on our buck pole, and looking back repeatedly at her as we drove out to resume hunting. I'll never forget my happiness when we returned hours later to find her still there!

Nor will I forget the scenes in camp that night as Dad's hunting partners took turns congratulating me on my deer. During supper they had me tell how I'd shot the doe. I remember Clayton, Fred, Jerry, Bozo, Adam, Hank, Rollie, Herbie, Wilbur and Duane

Just like his father, the author's son Jake got his start on forest whitetails during Wisconsin's nine-day firearms season.

217

The author developed his passion for big-woods bowhunting in the mid-1970s. In the decades since, he has been lucky to have friends and family who shared that passion.

listening with intense sincerity. It was a special moment indeed.

A couple of days later we removed my deer from the buck pole and registered it in town. We then hauled it back to camp where we skinned and quartered it. After supper, the group quickly reduced my first deer to venison. The butchering was another first for me. I was amazed how expertly Dad and his partners cut up and wrapped the deer. They used every scrap of meat they cut from the carcass. Some of it went for steaks, some for roasts and some for ground meat. We mixed the ground portions with seasonings and ground pork to make breakfast sausage.

We then used some of the venison for "camp meat" the next few days. I don't know if it was because the venison was from my own deer or if it was because it was so fresh, but that was the tastiest meat I had ever eaten. Perhaps it was a bit of both.

LIFE IN A DEER CAMP

As I learned the next six years, life in a big-woods deer camp was special. From the camaraderie to the nonsense, from the early-morning risings to the all-day hunts, from the special "Up North" food to the many hunting tales told 'round the supper table, I loved every minute. Our camp was as much a part of deer hunting as the deer themselves.

In December 1970, about six years after my first hunt in camp, I left home for a four-year hitch in the U.S. Air Force. I knew I would miss my family and friends, but I had no idea how much I would also miss my annual treks to our North Woods deer camp. Nor did I know how much our camp would change in my absence. Hank and Adam died. My grandpa, Fred Boese, became too crippled to make it to deer camp. Jerry developed serious health problems, and Duane bought a camp of his own. Bozo no longer went north for deer season, and Rollie hunted near home with two of his sons and his daughter. Even Dad gave up hunting the Northern forests.

When I returned, something happened to me, too. I developed an intense passion for bowhunting whitetails, and I wasn't alone in that love. Several longtime friends were also obsessed with chasing deer with the "stick and string." It was only logical that we turned our attentions to northwestern Wisconsin's forests. In 1975 my brother Mike and three of his buddies bought a cabin a mile from dad's deer camp, and a couple of years later I bought out one of the cabin's original shareholders. The stage was set for our own "Up-North" bowhunting camp.

Unlike Dad's camp, which was limited to the nine-day gun season each year, our bowhunting camp was a hub of activity every weekend throughout the three-month archery season. In addition, some of us spent a week at the cabin during the rut's peak in early November. Those were some of the most memorable bowhunting experiences I enjoyed during my first 40 years in the sport. In fact, the memories I cherish most came from deer camp. Our core group of bowhunters included my brothers Mike, Jim and Jeff; and friends Mike, Gabby, Rabs, Mac and Rod. We also entertained guests just about every weekend. It wasn't unusual to have as many as 12 bowhunters in camp on any given weekend.

Some readers might wonder how we found enough good hunting spots for so many bowhunters. That was really no problem. We had more than a million acres of public land in three counties at our disposal, so we barely scratched the surface of the land available to us. In fact, during most seasons we ran out of time long before we ran out of places to hunt. It remains that way today in many forests across the Great Lakes states.

Not until our big-woods bow camp began dissolving years later did I appreciate what a special group we assembled. We had great cooks and great eaters. We had pranksters and no-non-

This photo, taken during Wisconsin's gun season, shows the author with some of the guys who became members of his North Woods bowhunting camp.

sense guys. We had great hunters and guys who didn't care if they saw a deer. The one trait we all shared was our enjoyment of getting away "Up North."

BENEFITS OF HUNTING WITH A GROUP

As it had been with Dad's camp, our crew enjoyed sharing hunting stories. We met back at camp around midmorning, devoured a huge breakfast, and then shared our experiences from the morning's hunts. We also decided who would help when trailing jobs were needed.

That routine was much the same at night. We met at the cabin after hunting and discussed the day's hunts over supper. If someone shot a deer during the evening hunt we discussed the situation and debated whether to trail the deer with lanterns or wait until morning to go. In looking back, I better realize the advantage of discussing trailing situations with other experienced bowhunters. For instance, I learned this rule: "When in doubt, back out." I can only guess how many marginally hit deer we recovered because someone was adamant about waiting longer.

We also recovered many deer because of the camp's never-say-die attitude. Everyone had helped on many blood-trailing jobs, and we knew from experience that a sparse blood trail didn't always mean a superficial hit. One particular incident in the late 1970s illustrates that point. Just after first light on a snappy-cold day in early November, one of the guys arrowed a buck.

The author's hundreds of experiences trailing wounded deer with camp members taught him that, in most cases, two or three talented trackers are more effective than 10 or more neophytes.

221

Unfortunately, the buck took a step just as he released his arrow, so the broadhead center-shot the liver. He and another member of our group took up the buck's trail and followed it more than a mile before returning to camp.

"We left him where he crossed a logging trail," my partner said. "He bled good at first, but now he's leaving only a drop every 20 yards or so. We were struggling to follow him, so we thought we'd grab some lunch and go back out. We could sure use another set of eyes."

I agreed to help, and 20 minutes later we stood where the buck crossed the logging trail. The blood trail was bleak. In fact, we spent a half-hour trying to find the next drop of blood and nearly 15 minutes to find the one that followed. As it turned out, that's all we needed. I was a bit in front of my partners when I spotted the buck lying dead in a depression 30 yards ahead. That rutting buck had made it more than a mile after the hit.

I recall other instances when it took the entire camp to find a wounded whitetail. I don't usually favor having eight or 10 people on a trailing job. In fact, my hundreds of experiences trailing wounded deer taught me that two or three veteran trackers are usually more effective than 10 or more inexperienced trackers. In some cases, however, it's a big advantage to have many eyes working on the recovery. This approach works best when you've lost a blood trail completely, like when rain or snow wipes out the trail.

In those cases, our group returned to where we last found blood, and used the spot as a hub for our grid search. When doing these searches we assumed we wouldn't find a blood trail. We were looking for a body. Once centered, we spread out with equal numbers on each side of the hub. We stayed just far enough apart so we could see the trackers on both sides of us. Then, once we were lined up, we walked straight ahead, making sure to stay in a straight line. After walking perhaps several hundred yards, we stopped, regrouped and spread out again left or right of where we just walked. The outside man always stayed as close as possible to the deer's last known line of travel, and then returned slowly to the original starting point. At that point we turned and performed the same grid search on the side we hadn't covered.

Again, I feel blessed because every guy in that big-woods bowhunting camp was an excellent woodsman. They not only

Hanging around top-notch bowhunters in a camp will always make you a better bowhunter if you pay attention. That's the kind of jump-start the author enjoyed when he started bowhunting.

knew what to look for when blood-trailing, they also knew where to look for it. Just as importantly, they knew it was vital to move slowly when searching for a body. In the years since our group disbanded, I appreciate their skills even more. I've rarely seen such skills displayed in recent years.

A RARE BREED INDEED

I find it interesting that our bowhunting camp ran so well with little planning. From what I remember, none of our eight to 10 guys took time to coordinate our weekend hunts. We simply showed up on Friday night, downed a couple of "cold ones," briefly discussed our plans for morning, and then hit the rack. We were out of bed well before daylight the next day to drink a little coffee and review our plans a bit more. These talks occasionally inspired a last-minute change for someone, but for the most part, our minds were made up in advance. The only thing that forced a change was a sudden shift in wind direction.

When I reflect on those strategy sessions, I better understand where I gained most of my deer hunting knowledge. My bowhunting camp played a huge role in making me consistently successful. I couldn't have asked for better teachers. Thanks to their skills, I also got a jump-start in my development as an archer and whitetail educator. For instance, one member of our group was a state champion in archery. He provided priceless advice on how to improve my shooting. Another member had unbelievable trailing skills, and yet another had an uncanny ability to read the woods for whitetail patterns. Another guy, in particular, knew far more than the rest of us about what made mature bucks tick.

I quizzed these guys whenever possible and steadily gained a better-rounded understanding of what it took to become a big-woods bowhunter. Most importantly, I learned we can never truly know everything about big white-tailed bucks. The learning process continues until we quit bowhunting.

Another interesting thing about our camp was the bond between the members, even though we seldom saw or talked with each other during the week. Not only did we talk about bowhunting for whitetails, we also discussed almost everything in our lives. I found it similar to friendships I established during my tour of duty in Vietnam, especially the fact we trusted each other so much. Together, we shared the joys and celebrations of successful hunts, as well as the frustrations and disappointments of hunts that went awry.

Our group also had an unexplainable "feel" for each other while in the woods. Whether we were scouting for new stands, trailing a wounded deer, or exploring new country, we seemed to communicate without speaking. I guess after bowhunting together for years, you learn each other's tendencies as each day unfolds. I remember several instances when I'd be walking and scouting in the forest with one or more of my camp partners and then lose track of them for a long time. Somehow we usually reunited without planning it. We'd look at each other, grin, and say something like, "I guess we got pulled to the same spot."

SUMMARY

It's difficult to write about my bowhunting camp without thinking of my parents, grandparents and other elders in my life, and all their conversations about the good old days. I guess I've now reached the age where I can talk about and remember

The author hopes he can someday pass along to his son the many great traditions and unforgettable moments that come from being part of a big-woods bowhunting camp.

my own good old days, especially where big-woods bowhunting camps are concerned.

I'll never forget the great atmosphere and good times in my dad's deer camp in the mid-1960s. I also remember similar good times in my own big-woods bowhunting camp during the mid-1970s to early 1980s. I doubt those memories will ever be dulled by the passing years. I can only hope that someday, somehow, I can pass along to my children the great traditions and unforgettable moments that come from sharing a bow camp in the big woods.

225

CHAPTER EIGHTEEN

THE FOREST AT SUNSET

I had been on my stand since before dawn, and it was now 9:30 a.m. Had this been a bit later in the season I wouldn't have considered ending my morning hunt so early, but the rut was still a good two weeks away. With bucks entrenched in their dreaded "October lull," I knew there was little chance of seeing any antlers this late in the morning. I quietly gathered my gear and climbed down from my portable stand.

That morning's only action had occurred about 15 minutes after daylight when a doe with twin fawns walked by. They were followed a few minutes later by a spike buck. The spike had just disappeared into a tamarack swamp when I heard another deer on the same trail. A single, subtle grunt tipped me off that this deer also was a buck. I grabbed my bow from its hanger and got into position to shoot. Before long I made out the form of a whitetail approaching through some thick dogwoods. One glance told me the buck wasn't a shooter. The forkhorn passed within 15 yards of me, just as the others had. That was it for the morning's action.

My son, Jake, was waiting at the pickup when I walked out. He had also seen a short flurry of activity at dawn. Unlike me, however, Jake had seen a monster buck. He believed it was the same deer he had seen on two previous hunts.

"He was walking behind a herd of does and fawns," Jake said. "He was about 50 yards away, and I blew my grunt call a couple

The author's son, Jake, will never forget a close encounter in the big woods one early October. A monster buck approached, looked his way, but then turned and followed the other deer into a swamp.

of times to try to get him closer. He looked my way, but then turned and followed the other deer toward the swamp."

That bowhunt took place several years ago in a forested region of north-central Wisconsin. I'm sad to say that was one of the last forest bowhunts Jake and I did together. Circumstances brought about by poor political decisions prevented us from returning to the North Woods. In brief, state legislators forced our wildlife agency to make deer baiting legal in Wisconsin unless chronic wasting disease or tuberculosis is found nearby. That risky decision ensured North Woods deer would set their feeding clock according to artificial food sources, a practice that increases the likelihood of food-contamination and disease outbreaks, not to mention disrupting their natural foraging routines.

MORE THAN JUST KILLING A BUCK

More on that later. When I reflect on all my years of hunting forests and deep woods, I try to emphasize the positive. After all, I've had the great fortune of bowhunting more than a dozen states and two provinces in search of big white-tailed bucks. Those bowhunts have provided a wealth of unforgettable memories — some pleasant and some not so pleasant. I find it almost amazing that many of my most special memories don't involve a dead deer.

One of my fondest memories involves a hunt for shed antlers in northwestern Wisconsin in the mid-1980s. Now, I realize modern-day bowhunters might think they're pioneers in shed-hunting, but this activity is hardly new. A man from Minnesota named Lee Murphy is a true shed-hunting pioneer, and my big-woods bowhunting partners and I have long hunted sheds as part of our routine. One day in March years ago, my brother Jeff and our mutual friend Dan Dyson were scouring a huge tract of land that included hardwood ridges interspersed with tamarack and alder swamps.

Jeff and I had walked part of the area the previous December, and discovered two important facts. First, good numbers of deer were wintering in the area. Second, judging by the number of huge, fresh rubs we found, several mature bucks were around. During our March visit, Dan, Jeff and I split up, each of

228

This photo shows a small part of the author's collection of big-woods shed antlers he and his group picked up during the mid-1980s. He believes few of these bucks were ever killed by hunters.

229

The author poses with a hunting partner, Dan Dyson, and two matched sets of shed antlers from the same buck. Unbelievably, the author and Dyson found the four antlers the same day.

us targeting a specific area. We had been in the woods only about 30 minutes when Dan hollered that he'd found a couple of antlers. One of them undoubtedly was from a 2½-year-old buck. The other antler, however, was the massive 5-point right beam from a mature buck. Judging by their bleached and slightly chewed condition, the antlers had lain in the woods since the previous year.

We found six more antlers that day, including this highlight: Dan found the matching left antler to the massive 5-point beam. Perhaps even more unbelievably, I found that same buck's matched set of fresh sheds the same day! The four antlers were so similar in size and configuration that it looked as though they had been formed from a mold. The only noticeable difference between the sets was that Dan's were more sun-bleached than mine. That was one of our first shed-antler hunts, and we capped it off by finding single sheds from three other "shooter" bucks. As you might have guessed, those finds prompted me to bowhunt that area fairly hard the following autumn. Although I didn't arrow that trophy, he provided some incredible memories.

The most special memory occurred on a cold, gray morning in early November when I heard the buck grunting steadily and breaking brush as it approached. The brute finally appeared 15 yards from my stand. Unfortunately, a patch of brush prevented me from directing an arrow to his vitals. He eventually figured out something wasn't right and bounded away. That buck fell to a gun-hunter a couple of weeks later. Along with his massive 10-point typical frame, the buck had grown short, matching drop tines off both beams. He had also sprouted matching 3-inch stickers off his G-2 tines. His Boone and Crockett score netted about 185 nontypical points.

I admit I was initially devastated to hear someone else had shot "my" buck, but my "depression" lasted only a few months. As we had done the previous March, Dan, Jeff and I returned to the buck's old stomping grounds to hunt sheds. We were in the woods only a few minutes when I picked up a fresh shed. Though not nearly as massive as the matched sheds we had found the year before, the 5-point antler had extremely long tines and a long, sweeping main beam. My educated guess was that the buck was 3½ years old.

Granted, my heart still ached that the "shed-horn buck" was dead, but I now held proof that another stud buck was "in the works." I figured he would be impressive by autumn. Winter that year had been mild, and the forest had also produced an excellent acorn crop the previous fall. Those factors made it certain the buck would add a lot more inches to an already impressive set of antlers.

To be honest, though, I wasn't surprised. In fact, I had come to expect such surprises when hunting forests and deep woods. I had long ago realized that when one monster buck disappears, another is usually lurking, ready to take its place. The dozens of shed antlers we found over the years proved proof-positive that a "reserve pool" of trophy bucks was always under development.

Here's what the "shed-horn buck" grew into the year after the author and Dan Dyson picked up two of its matched sets of sheds. The rack scored in the mid-180s as a nontypical.

Even so, we tried to keep track of as many individual big bucks as possible. My big-woods hunting partners and I knew just about every bowhunter near us. We also kept a close eye on buck poles at every deer camp during gun season. If anyone nearby killed a big buck during the bow or gun seasons, we knew about it almost instantly.

BIG-WOODS BUCKS ARE SPECIAL!

Our running inventory of harvested bucks provided some interesting information. For instance, of the shed antlers we found, less than one-third of the bucks that grew them were ever killed by hunters. Even more interesting was that we had no sheds or other previous knowledge of several big bucks killed around us each year. We found that fact humbling because my partners and I spent enormous amounts of time scouting, hunting and looking for shed antlers in the very areas where many of those big bucks fell. We prided ourselves on having a decent handle on big bucks in our areas, yet every year someone shot a bruiser that was a stranger to us.

It took a few years, but we finally conceded that no matter how hard we worked, we could never acquire firsthand knowledge of every big buck living in a given area. That's just the way it is in forests and deep woods. The country is too vast and the deer too wary to make anything besides a partial census of mature bucks. Then again, I take comfort knowing some whitetails can escape detection by even the best hunters. I guess that's why I so love the big-woods challenge and, after hunting nearly every habitat known to whitetails, still find myself returning to the big timber.

The bowhunt that captures the essence of my big-woods fascination occurred in 1980. To reach the area, I first had to navigate my four-wheel-drive vehicle about a half-mile down a muddy logging trail. I then had about 15 minutes of hard walking to reach my stand. The rewards were worth the effort, however. This area held a small pocket of red oaks surrounded by hundreds of acres of poplar, birch and maple. The red oaks that autumn were loaded with acorns. The deer bedded in the outlying hardwoods and then moved toward the oaks early in the evening to feed. They also passed through the oaks in the morn-

233

ing to gobble up acorns before bedding for the day.

I had hunted inside the oaks off and on since the bow season opened in mid-September. I had seen dozens of deer, including several shooters. Try as I might, however, I couldn't seem to get my stands dialed into the right spots. As the acorn supply dwindled, the whitetails restricted their feeding efforts to a few select spots.

When hunting the morning of Nov. 1, I saw a bunch of antlerless deer and several small bucks the first hour. They eventually moved off, and everything was quiet for 10 minutes. Then I heard the unmistakable sounds of a deer walking deliberately toward the oaks. Just as I grabbed my bow from its hanger, the deer walked into sight. I didn't need a second look to confirm it was a shooter. The big deer walked to the spot 50 yards away where the antlerless deer and small bucks had fed. The hog-bodied 8-pointer nosed around for a few minutes and then gorged on acorns for nearly 10 minutes. He then snapped his head erect, looked around, and walked away in the direction the other deer had gone.

I waited 30 minutes before climbing down and repositioning my stand in a large red oak 15 yards from where the deer had fed. I then returned around midafternoon and spent two hours watching squirrels finding and burying acorns. The first deer, a doe and fawn, didn't show up until 15 minutes before dark. Right away, I knew something was up. The doe and fawn trotted to within a few yards of my tree before stopping to look at their back-trail. Seconds later I heard a loud grunt, and then the big buck from that morning walked stiff-legged into view. I just knew he would follow the two antlerless deer past my stand.

That's not quite what happened. When the brute was perhaps 40 yards away he stopped and thrashed a 4-inch diameter maple tree. He continued to work out on the tree until dark. I waited until I could no longer see the buck, and then slipped out quietly.

I was back up that tree the next morning. A small 6-pointer appeared just after daylight, dined nearby on acorns for a few minutes, and then walked off toward the bedding area. Other than foraging squirrels, the oaks drew no further activity until

It took the author and his partners a few years to realize that no matter how hard they worked at it, they would never acquire firsthand knowledge of every big buck living in a given area.

During one especially memorable bowhunt, the author watched and heard a buck rubbing a tree out of bow range until it was swallowed up by darkness. All the author could do was wait several minutes before climbing down and walking out.

9:30 a.m. That's when the big buck reappeared. Just as he'd done the previous morning, the trophy deer strode into the oaks and sniffed the ground where the small buck had fed 15 yards away.

After releasing my arrow, I felt confident I had made a good hit. Instead of taking up the trail, however, I returned to camp for assistance. Man, was I glad I did! As it turned out, my brother Jeff — who was only 12 at the time — and my good friend, Swede, were waiting there. Their assistance with the trailing job only created more vivid memories of the day.

The buck fell nearly a half-mile from the logging trail where I parked my vehicle. Jeff was too small to be of much help dragging out the buck, so we gave him our bows and told him to walk ahead 100 yards or so and wait for us to catch up. Just before he took off I reminded him to "keep walking toward the sun" to find the nearby logging trail.

Somehow, Jeff misunderstood my instructions. Swede and I dragged the buck a good 100 yards, but saw no sign of Jeff. Worse, we heard no reply when we hollered. I panicked, of course. I instantly assumed Jeff had gotten off course and was hopelessly lost in the forest. How the heck would I explain to Mom and Dad that I had misplaced their baby boy?

"Well, we might as well keep dragging your buck to the logging trail," Swede said. "We'll keep hollering as we go, and maybe he'll hear us. If he doesn't, we'll go get some help."

Swede and I finally reached the logging trail. Lo and behold, Jeff was sitting on a stump by the trail! Apparently the wind was blowing just hard enough to keep him from hearing us when we called for him. I was doubly relieved. We'd found my little brother, and the buck was out of the woods.

THE PASSION BURNS, BUT ...

I wish I could report that Wisconsin continues to provide the bulk of my big-woods bowhunting experiences. Unfortunately, that isn't the case. Earlier, I mentioned that deer baiting has prevented my son and me from doing much bowhunting in my home state's North Woods since the late 1990s. Those who know me also know I vehemently oppose baiting. I think it's bad for the deer, and it's bad for hunters and the future of hunting.

Hunting should involve much more than dumping a pile of

237

corn and waiting for a big buck to show up. It cheapens wildlife and the hunting experience. Big-woods bowhunting should require hours and days of scouting and map/photo research, as well as countless miles of legwork. It should also require that we learn which naturally growing foods attract big-woods deer at specific times of the season. And finally, it should require that we try to discover how to exploit the habits and travel patterns of big-woods deer using natural food sources, not artificial feed dumps. If I can decipher the woods, everyone can. Unfortunately, I reaped the benefits of all my hard work only a few seasons before baiters moved into my favorite big-woods hunting area in the 1990s.

The sudden appearance of corn piles throughout the forest changed the habits and travel patterns of its deer. Equally bad, baiting made many Wisconsin deer hunters become lazy, both physically and mentally, disconnecting them from the forest itself. A disconnected hunter can never become a skilled, astute observer of white-tailed deer behavior. I hate to say it, but the arts of scouting and interpreting deer sign are disappearing in my home state.

In fact, baiting became so widespread that I eventually sold my share of my hunting cabin in northwestern Wisconsin. With that sale, the Miller family's long-time tradition of chasing big-woods whitetails came to an end. However, my son and I would return to those forests in a heartbeat if baiting were banned.

I've heard every so-called argument used by baiters to futilely defend the practice. Some claim baiting is the only way to ensure their kids see deer every time out. Others claim baiting is a necessity for older deer-camp members. Still others claim it's impossible to kill mature bucks without bait. I must say that's all hogwash.

Baiting forced me to travel to bowhunt states where baiting is illegal. Funny, I never hear residents in those states complaining that their kids and/or older bowhunters don't see enough deer. And I never hear big-woods bowhunters in those states complain that it's impossible to kill mature bucks without bait. Their photos prove otherwise. Their states have never allowed the practice.

One thing I hear bowhunters from other states complain

The author worries that deer baiting has already produced an entire generation of disconnected hunters in Wisconsin and Michigan. He longs for the bygone days when fathers took along their sons and daughters and taught them how to "read the woods" when bowhunting forest deer.

about, however, is the impact baiting has had on Wisconsin's bowhunters. Not long ago, these North Woods bowhunters were respected as some of the most hard-working and knowledgeable in North America. Sadly, that's no longer the case. When people I visit now ask about Wisconsin, they assume everyone is baiting, and their lack of respect for big bucks killed in my state is obvious.

What does the future hold for me and my family's love for bowhunting big-woods whitetails? Well, as long as baiting is legal in my state, I won't waste a second bowhunting our North Woods. I'll continue to hold out hope that lawmakers will one day realize how baiting and feeding deer ruins the hunt and jeopardizes the deer themselves. Until that revelation occurs, I'll jump at every chance to hunt other forests and deep-woods regions where I can pit my skills against whitetails under totally fair-chase conditions.

Hey, no bait, no problem! If your state doesn't allow baiting, I urge you to work steadfastly to keep it out of your deer woods. I can assure you, once it's allowed in, you'll witness a monster that ignores facts and insists everyone hunt with a bow or gun in one hand, and a corn bucket in the other. What kind of heritage is that to pass along?

But I won't end this book on a sour note. If you've read this far, you know my love for bowhunting the forests and deep woods for whitetails will never burn out. Maybe that's why I feel such profound disappointment when realizing how much Jake and I lost when this indefensible practice turned deer hunting and deer behavior on its ear. Fortunately, few other regions except Michigan's North Woods also experience widespread baiting. Therefore, bowhunters can usually expect great deer hunting and intense challenges every time we put the road behind us and walk alone into these large, sprawling, quiet expanses. Believe me, no better experience can be had with the bow and arrow.